Praise for BILLIC

'Gripping and necessary...some of the be:
read...made indelible by his low-key, acerbi
remarkable, varied, and always on puirm.'
Jeet Heer, *The Nation*

'I am a big fan. I'm always in awe of the amount of information that Darryl
manages to pack in to every one of his comic books.'
Robin Ince

'Cunningham's nonfiction work is undoubtedly some of the most crucially
important practice to have emerged in UK comics in the last decade.'
Andy Oliver, *Broken Frontier*

'A beautifully drawn exposé of the men who burnt the planet. Each picture
is worth far more than a thousand complex academic words.'
Danny Dorling

Praise for SUPERCRASH

'A hugely readable, revelatory condemnation and call to arms.'
The Independent

'A remarkable read, visually clever and inventive...eminently readable.'
Forbidden Planet

'Cunningham's pithy prose and funky art tell a complex, important tale...
tackling tangled subjects with clarity and zing.'
Michael Goodwin, author of *Economix*

'Provocative, thoughtful... *Supercrash* will leave you better informed and,
more than that, it will leave you angry.'
Teddy Jamieson, *Herald Scotland*

'Decodes the ideas with virtuosity...'
L'Humanité

'A truly outstanding piece of work, illustrated so intelligently in his
wonderful no-nonsense informative style.'
Page 45

Praise for SCIENCE TALES

Praise for GRAPHIC SCIENCE

DARRYL CUNNINGHAM
PUTIN & RUSSIA
THE RISE OF A DICTATOR

First published in 2021 by
Myriad Editions
www.myriadeditions.com

Myriad Editions
An imprint of New Internationalist Publications
The Old Music Hall, 106–108 Cowley Rd,
Oxford OX4 1JE

First printing
1 3 5 7 9 10 8 6 4 2

A CIP catalogue record for this book is available from
the British Library

ISBN: 978-1-912408-91-7
E-ISBN: 978-1-912408-92-4

Printed in Poland
www.lfbookservices.co.uk

VLADIMIR VLADIMIROVICH PUTIN

BORN IN 1952, PUTIN GREW UP IN A COMMUNAL APARTMENT SHARED BY THREE FAMILIES IN ST PETERSBURG, THEN KNOWN AS LENINGRAD. JUST EIGHT YEARS HAD PASSED SINCE THE END OF THE SIEGE OF LENINGRAD, IN WHICH MORE THAN A MILLION OF THE CITY'S INHABITANTS HAD DIED, KILLED BY HUNGER OR BY ARTILLERY FIRE.

MUCH OF WHAT WE KNOW ABOUT PUTIN'S EARLY LIFE COMES FROM A SERIES OF INTERVIEWS HE GAVE IN 2000, PUBLISHED IN THE BOOK *FIRST PERSON*, WHICH IS PERHAPS AS MUCH AN ATTEMPT BY HIM AT MYTH-MAKING AS IT IS AN ENTIRELY TRUE ACCOUNT. THIS SHOULD BE KEPT IN MIND WHEN YOU READ THE FOLLOWING.

BEFORE THE WAR, THE ELDER PUTIN, ALSO NAMED VLADIMIR, HAD BEEN A CONSCRIPT IN THE SOVIET NAVY, SERVING IN THE SUBMARINE FLEET IN THE EARLY 1930s.

AS SOON AS THE WAR BEGAN HE JOINED THE DESTRUCTION BATTALION OF THE NKVD (A SECRET POLICE AGENCY ORIGINALLY TASKED WITH CONDUCTING REGULAR POLICE WORK AND OVERSEEING THE COUNTRY'S PRISONS AND LABOUR CAMPS). LATER, HE WAS TRANSFERRED TO THE REGULAR ARMY WHERE HE WAS SEVERELY WOUNDED, HIS LEGS BLASTED BY A GERMAN GRENADE.

PUTIN'S FATHER SURVIVED, BUT HE WAS IN HOSPITAL FOR MONTHS. HIS WIFE FOUND HIM AND VISITED HIM THERE EVERY DAY.

THE ELDER PUTIN SAW THAT HIS WIFE WAS HALF DEAD FROM STARVATION, SO HE BEGAN TO GIVE HER HIS OWN FOOD, MAKING SURE THE NURSES DIDN'T SEE THIS.

BUT WHEN THE DOCTORS SAW VLADIMIR FAINTING FROM HUNGER, THEY SOON REALISED WHAT HE'D BEEN DOING.

HE GOT A STERN LECTURE AND WAS BANNED FROM SEEING HIS WIFE FOR A WHILE.

HOWEVER, BOTH OF PUTIN'S PARENTS SURVIVED THE WAR, ALTHOUGH HIS FATHER'S INJURIES LEFT HIM WITH A LIFELONG LIMP.

THE YOUNG PUTIN GREW UP IN THE TRASH-STREWN, RAT-INFESTED COURTYARDS OF THE CITY'S APARTMENT BLOCKS. YOUNGER AND SLIGHTER OF BUILD THAN THE OTHER BOYS, HE HELD HIS OWN. HIS FORMER CLASSMATE AND LONG-TIME FRIEND, VIKTOR BORISENKO, RECALLS THAT IF YOUNG PUTIN WAS EVER INSULTED, HE WOULD FIGHT FEROCIOUSLY, BITING AND SCRATCHING, USING ANY DIRTY METHOD TO TAKE VENGEANCE ON ANYONE WHO ATTEMPTED TO HUMILIATE HIM.

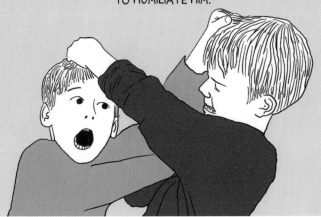

AFTER THE WAR PUTIN'S FATHER WORKED
AT THE YEGOROV FACTORY, WHICH BUILT
PASSENGER CARRIAGES FOR THE SOVIET UNION'S
RAILWAY SYSTEM. WHETHER HE REMAINED
A RESERVE MEMBER OF THE SECRET POLICE
(KNOWN BY THEN AS THE KGB) IS A MATTER OF
CONJECTURE. MANY THOUSANDS OF OFFICERS
HELD REGULAR JOBS WHILE ALSO INFORMING FOR,
AND DRAWING A SALARY FROM, THE KGB. THIS MAY
EXPLAIN WHY THE PUTINS LIVED COMPARATIVELY
WELL: THEY HAD A TELEVISION AND A TELEPHONE,
RARE ITEMS FOR ORDINARY SOVIET PEOPLE
AT THIS TIME.

IN 1964, THE YOUNGER
PUTIN TOOK UP SAMBO, A
SOVIET MARTIAL ART
THAT MIXED JUDO AND
WRESTLING, AND WAS SUITED
TO HIS SMALL STATURE AND
TOUGH NATURE.

SAMBO, WITH ITS DISCIPLINE, BECAME
PART OF PUTIN'S TRANSFORMATION FROM
ACADEMICALLY POOR STREET THUG INTO
A GOAL-DIRECTED AND HARD-WORKING
ADOLESCENT. IT WAS HIS AMBITION TO JOIN
THE KGB AND HE HAD HEARD THAT THEY
EXPECTED NEW RECRUITS TO BE SKILLED IN
HAND-TO-HAND COMBAT.

AT THE AGE OF 16, A YEAR BEFORE FINISHING SECONDARY SCHOOL, PUTIN WENT TO THE KGB HEADQUARTERS IN LENINGRAD. THE PLACE HAD AN EVIL REPUTATION, HAVING BEEN THE OFFICES OF STALIN'S SECRET POLICE, WHERE SUPPOSED ENEMIES OF THE STATE HAD BEEN EXECUTED IN BLOOD-DRENCHED BASEMENT ROOMS.

HE ASKED THE OFFICER WHO SAW HIM THERE WHAT HE WOULD HAVE TO DO JOIN THE KGB AND WAS TOLD THAT HE WOULD HAVE TO EITHER DO MILITARY SERVICE OR GRADUATE FROM UNIVERSITY FIRST.

SO, THE FIERCELY DETERMINED PUTIN WENT TO LENINGRAD STATE UNIVERSITY AND GRADUATED WITH A LAW DEGREE IN 1975.

ALL THROUGH THE YEARS HE SPENT AT UNIVERSITY, PUTIN WAITED FOR THE MAN HE SPOKE TO AT KGB HEADQUARTERS TO GET IN TOUCH WITH HIM. BUT THERE WAS ONLY SILENCE. HE MADE NO MOVES HIMSELF, BECAUSE HE KNEW THEY DIDN'T SIGN UP VOLUNTEERS.

BUT THEN OUT OF THE BLUE HE WAS CONTACTED BY A MAN WHO WANTED TO MEET HIM. THE MAN DID NOT SAY WHO HE WAS.

PUTIN RECALLED THE MAN TELLING HIM THAT THE DISCUSSION WOULD BE ABOUT FUTURE JOB ASSIGNMENTS, BUT HE REFUSED TO BE SPECIFIC.

THAT'S WHEN PUTIN REALISED THAT IF HE DIDN'T WANT TO SAY HE WORKED FOR THE KGB, THEN THAT MEANT HE DID.

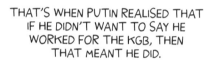

1975. HE JOINED THE KGB.

IF PUTIN EXPECTED A HIGH-OCTANE LIFE OF ADVENTURE, THEN HE MUST HAVE BEEN DISAPPOINTED. KGB LIFE IN A BACKWATER LIKE LENINGRAD MOSTLY INVOLVED PUSHING PAPER AROUND. AT THAT TIME, HE WAS JUST ONE OF MANY THOUSANDS OF YOUNG MEN WHO SWELLED THE BLOATED RANKS OF THE KGB WITH NO REAL PURPOSE.

AFTER TEN YEARS HE WAS TRANSFERRED TO THE KGB'S FOREIGN ESPIONAGE DIVISION AND POSTED TO DRESDEN IN COMMUNIST EAST GERMANY.

HERE PUTIN CLAIMED TO HAVE BEEN COLLATING RECORDS AND DEBRIEFING EAST GERMAN CITIZENS WHO TRAVELLED ABROAD.

HE HAD MARRIED LYUDMILA SHKREBNEVA, A DOMESTIC FLIGHT ATTENDANT FROM THE BALTIC SEA CITY OF KALININGRAD.

THE COUPLE HAD TWO CHILDREN, MARIA AND YEKATERINA.

IN HIS OFFICIAL BIOGRAPHY, PUTIN CLAIMS THAT, IN DRESDEN, DEPRESSED BY THE DULL ROUTINE OF HIS WORK, HE DRANK BEER, STOPPED EXERCISING, GOT FAT, AND DID NOTHING OF INTEREST.

URP!

THIS SEEMS VERY UNLIKELY. A FEW FACTS ARE KNOWN ABOUT WHAT PUTIN ACTUALLY DID DO IN DRESDEN.

HE WAS A LIAISON OFFICER WITH THE EAST GERMAN STASI (SECRET POLICE) AND HE WAS INVOLVED IN RECRUITING SCIENTISTS AND BUSINESSMEN WHO COULD HELP THE KGB SMUGGLE WESTERN TECHNOLOGY INTO THE EASTERN BLOC.

AT THAT TIME THE KGB HAD ASSETS OR AGENTS PLACED INSIDE MANY GERMAN COMPANIES, INCLUDING SIEMENS, BAYER, MESSERSCHMITT AND THYSSEN.

PUTIN ALSO HANDLED 'SLEEPER AGENTS' — SPIES WHO ARE PLACED IN A TARGET COUNTRY TO ACT AS POTENTIAL ASSETS IF ACTIVATED.

PUTIN CLEARLY ADMIRED THESE AGENTS, SAYING HE THOUGHT THEM UNIQUE IN BEING ABLE TO GIVE UP THEIR LIVES AND LOVED ONES...

AND LEAVE THE COUNTRY FOR MANY YEARS TO SERVE THE CAUSE OF THE SOVIET UNION. HE BELIEVED THAT ONLY AN ELITE COULD DO THIS.

MEANWHILE, THE SOVIET UNION WAS DISINTEGRATING. MIKHAIL SERGEYEVICH GORBACHEV, WHO HAD A DISTINCTIVE BIRTHMARK ON HIS HEAD, WAS THE EIGHTH AND LAST LEADER OF THE SOVIET UNION.

GORBACHEV'S MAIN DOMESTIC GOAL WAS TO REVIVE THE SOVIET ECONOMY AFTER ITS YEARS OF LOW GROWTH, DUE, IN LARGE PART, TO EXCESSIVE MILITARY SPENDING. HIS FOCUS WAS ON INCREASING WORKER PRODUCTIVITY, RAPIDLY MODERNISING TECHNOLOGY, AND TRANSFORMING OPPRESSIVE SOVIET BUREAUCRACY.

WHEN THESE CHANGES FAILED TO BRING RESULTS, GORBACHEV BEGAN DEEPER ECONOMIC AND POLITICAL SYSTEM REFORMS. HIS NEW POLICY, GLASNOST (MEANING 'OPENNESS'), INSTIGATED A MAJOR CULTURAL THAW.

WITH FREEDOMS AND INFORMATION GREATLY BROADENED, THE PRESS WERE SUDDENLY ALLOWED TO REPORT FRANKLY ON CURRENT EVENTS.

GORBACHEV'S NEW POLICY OF PERESTROIKA (RESTRUCTURING) WAS THE FIRST ATTEMPT AT DEMOCRATISING THE SOVIET POLITICAL SYSTEM.

BOTH SECRET BALLOTING AND MULTI-CANDIDATE CONTESTS WERE INTRODUCED IN SOME PARTY AND GOVERNMENT ELECTIONS.

GORBACHEV LARGELY AVOIDED THE TOTALITARIAN USE OF POWER, PREVIOUSLY USED TO CRUSH DISSENT AND FREE SPEECH.

BUT HE ALSO RESISTED ANY REAL SHIFT TO PRIVATE OWNERSHIP AND THE USE OF FREE-MARKET MECHANISMS.

AND SO THE CENTRALLY PLANNED ECONOMY CONTINUED TO CRUMBLE WITH NO PRIVATE ENTERPRISE TO REPLACE IT.

CHANGE SPREAD. IN LATE 1989-90, DEMOCRATICALLY ELECTED, NON-COMMUNIST GOVERNMENTS CAME TO POWER IN EAST GERMANY, POLAND, HUNGARY, AND CZECHOSLOVAKIA.

IN SOME OF RUSSIA'S CONSTITUENT REPUBLICS — INCLUDING GEORGIA, UZBEKISTAN AND AZERBAIJAN — THE NEW FREEDOMS ARISING FROM GORBACHEV'S DEMOCRATISATION OF THE POLITICAL SYSTEM LED TO CIVIL UNREST, AND, IN LITHUANIA, AN ATTEMPT TO GAIN ABSOLUTE INDEPENDENCE.

GORBACHEV RETALIATED WITH MILITARY FORCE, SUPRESSING INTER-ETHNIC CONFLICT IN SEVERAL OF THE REPUBLICS.

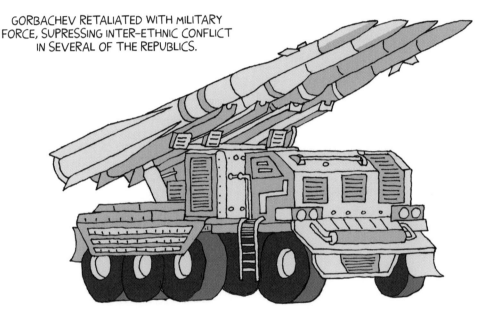

ON THE NIGHT OF 9 NOVEMBER 1989, CROWDS OF GERMANS BEGAN DISMANTLING THE BERLIN WALL, A BARRIER THAT FOR ALMOST 30 YEARS HAD SYMBOLISED THE COLD WAR DIVISION OF EUROPE.

BY OCTOBER 1990, GERMANY WAS REUNIFIED, TRIGGERING THE COLLAPSE OF THE OTHER EAST EUROPEAN REGIMES.

AFTER GERMANY WAS REUNIFIED, VLADIMIR PUTIN AND HIS WIFE LEFT DRESDEN AND RETURNED TO LENINGRAD.

PUBLICLY HE HAD RESIGNED FROM THE KGB WITH THE RANK OF LIEUTENANT COLONEL.

IN REALITY HE WAS MOST LIKELY ON THE KGB'S ACTIVE RESERVE LIST.

ONCE A SPY, ALWAYS A SPY.

HE GOT A JOB AS ASSISTANT TO THE CHANCELLOR FOR FOREIGN RELATIONS AT LENINGRAD STATE UNIVERSITY.

BUT HE WAS IN THAT POST FOR LESS THAN THREE MONTHS.

THEN HE CAME INTO THE ORBIT OF LAW PROFESSOR AND CELEBRITY POLITICIAN ANATOLY SOBCHAK.

SOBCHAK, A CHARISMATIC SPEAKER AND A FAMOUSLY SHARP DRESSER, HAD RIDDEN THE WAVE OF GORBACHEV-ERA DEMOCRACY REFORMS TO GAIN A POLITICAL FOOTHOLD IN THE CITY.

IN APRIL 1990, SOBCHAK WAS ELECTED A DEPUTY OF THE LENINGRAD CITY COUNCIL.

BY MAY HE WAS CHAIRMAN AND BY JUNE 1991 HE WAS MAYOR.

IT WAS AROUND THIS TIME THAT SOBCHAK RAN INTO PUTIN AT THE UNIVERSITY AND OFFERED HIM A JOB.

PUTIN

SPECULATION PERSISTED THAT PUTIN'S MOVE TO THE CITY ADMINISTRATION WAS ORCHESTRATED BY THE KGB, AND IT WAS FOR THIS REASON HE HAD RETURNED TO RUSSIA. A SPY USEFULLY POSTED AT THE HEART OF THE BURGEONING DEMOCRACY MOVEMENT.

SOBCHAK ALWAYS DENIED THAT THE KGB HAD ANYTHING TO DO WITH PUTIN'S APPOINTMENT.

PUTIN WASN'T ASSIGNED TO HIM BY THE KGB, SOBCHAK CLAIMED. HE SIMPLY REMEMBERED PUTIN, BOTH AS A STUDENT AND FOR HIS WORK AT THE LAW FACULTY.

WITH OR WITHOUT THE HELP OF THE KGB, BY 1991 PUTIN WAS WORKING FOR SOBCHAK IN THE NEW ADMINISTRATION.

ONE OF THE FACTORS THAT LED TO THE END OF THE SOVIET UNION WAS FOOD SHORTAGES.

THIS WAS A COUNTRY WHERE LONG LINES OUTSIDE STORES, HIGH PRICES AND ACUTE POVERTY WERE ENDEMIC.

THINGS WERE BETTER IN THE LARGER CITIES, BUT, EVEN SO, FROM JUNE 1989 LENINGRAD AUTHORITIES BEGAN RATIONING TEA AND SOAP.

FOUR MONTHS LATER, SUGAR, VODKA AND CIGARETTES JOINED THE LIST.

BY 1990, RATION CARDS WERE BEING ISSUED.

LENINGRAD CAME CLOSE TO MASS VIOLENCE TWICE IN 1990. THERE WAS A TOBACCO RIOT IN AUGUST...

...AND A FEW WEEKS LATER A SUGAR RIOT.

IT SHOULD HAVE BEEN A PRIORITY FOR LENINGRAD OFFICIALS TO GET FOOD INTO THE CITY, BUT THERE WERE PROBLEMS.

DURING THAT PERIOD A WOMAN CALLED MARINA SALYE WAS CHAIR OF THE CITY COUNCIL'S COMMITTEE ON FOOD SUPPLIES.

SHE NOTICED SOMETHING ODD ABOUT A CONSIGNMENT OF 60 TONS OF MEAT THAT THE CITY HAD ORDERED.

IT NEVER ARRIVED. SALYE CALLED SOBCHAK, WHO NAMED THE FIRM. SHE THEN CONFIRMED WITH THE BANK THAT A CREDIT LINE OF 90 MILLION DEUTSCHMARKS HAD BEEN OPENED FOR THIS FIRM.

SOBCHAK TOLD SALYE NOTHING ELSE, CLAIMING THAT HE HAD NO IDEA WHAT WAS GOING ON.

MARINA YEVGENYEVNA SALYE DID NOT INTEND TO BECOME A POLITICIAN.

A TALENTED SCIENTIST, SHE'D BEEN A DOCTOR OF GEOLOGY AND A RESEARCHER AT THE LENINGRAD INSTITUTE OF GEOLOGY.

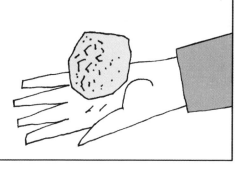

WHEN MIKHAIL GORBACHEV BEGAN HIS TENTATIVE EXPERIMENTS IN POLITICAL OPENNESS, SALYE EMERGED AS A LEADER OF A RADICAL GROUP OF ACTIVISTS.

SHE BECAME A PROMINENT MEMBER OF THE LENINGRAD PEOPLE'S FRONT AND WAS ELECTED TO THE CONGRESS OF PEOPLE'S DEPUTIES IN 1990.

IN THE POLITICAL TURMOIL OF THE FOLLOWING MONTHS, THERE WAS LITTLE TIME FOR SALYE TO PURSUE THE MATTER OF THE MISSING MEAT, BUT SHE DID NOT FORGET IT...

THE CHANGES THAT MIKHAIL GORBACHEV BROUGHT TO THE SOVIET
UNION WERE NOT JUST INTERNAL. IN DECEMBER 1987, HE SIGNED
AN AGREEMENT WITH THE US PRESIDENT RONALD REAGAN FOR THEIR
TWO COUNTRIES TO DESTROY ALL EXISTING STOCKS OF
INTERMEDIATE-RANGE NUCLEAR-TIPPED MISSILES. IN 1988-89, HE
OVERSAW THE WITHDRAWAL OF SOVIET TROOPS FROM AFGHANISTAN
AFTER THEIR NINE-YEAR OCCUPATION OF THAT COUNTRY.

YET ALTHOUGH GORBACHEV RECEIVED WIDESPREAD ACCLAIM
IN THE WEST FOR INSTIGATING SO MUCH CHANGE, HE WAS NOT
POPULAR BACK HOME. HARD-LINE COMMUNISTS FELT HE HAD
BETRAYED THE USSR, WHILE REFORMERS BELIEVED HE HAD NOT
GONE FAR ENOUGH. THE MAN WHO WOULD EVENTUALLY
USURP HIM WAS CALLED BORIS YELTSIN.

BORIS NIKOLAYEVICH YELTSIN WAS BORN IN A SMALL VILLAGE IN THE URAL MOUNTAINS IN 1931. AS A BOY, HE LOST TWO FINGERS FROM HIS LEFT HAND AFTER HE AND HIS FRIENDS PLAYED WITH GRENADES THEY HAD STOLEN FROM AN ARMY STORE.

BLAM!

AFTER YEARS WORKING FOR THE COMMUNIST PARTY, YELTSIN FIRST CAME TO PUBLIC ATTENTION IN 1985, WHEN GORBACHEV BROUGHT HIM TO MOSCOW. THERE, HE TOOK ON THE TASK OF CLEANING OUT CORRUPTION IN THE MOSCOW PARTY ORGANISATION.

YOW!

IN HIS ROLE AS FIRST SECRETARY OF MOSCOW'S COMMUNIST PARTY COMMITTEE, HE WAS EFFECTIVELY MAYOR OF THE SOVIET CAPITAL.

IN 1986, HE WAS ELEVATED TO THE POLITBURO (THE PRINCIPAL POLICY MAKING COMMITTEE IN THE SOVIET UNION) AS A NON-VOTING MEMBER.

КПСС

DESPITE THE INITIAL PATRONAGE, YELTSIN WAS IN NO WAY GORBACHEV'S MAN. HE SOON CAME INTO CONFLICT WITH THE SOVIET LEADER...

YELTSIN!

...AFTER HE CRITICISED THE SLOW PACE OF ECONOMIC REFORM, AND EVEN GORBACHEV HIMSELF...

WHAT DID YOU SAY ABOUT ME?

HUMPH!

YELTSIN WAS FORCED TO RESIGN FROM THE MOSCOW PARTY LEADERSHIP IN 1987 AND FROM THE POLITBURO A YEAR LATER.

HE WAS DEMOTED TO A DEPUTY MINISTER FOR CONSTRUCTION. THIS MIGHT HAVE BEEN THE END OF HIM, BUT HE THEN STAGED A REMARKABLE COMEBACK. HE HAD REMAINED POPULAR WITH SOVIET VOTERS, AND, BECAUSE OF THIS, IN MARCH 1989, HE WAS ABLE TO WIN A SEAT IN THE CONGRESS OF PEOPLE'S DEPUTIES (THE NEW SOVIET PARLIAMENT), WITH A LANDSLIDE VOTE.

A YEAR LATER, ON 29 MAY 1990, THE RUSSIAN PARLIAMENT ELECTED HIM PRESIDENT OF THE RUSSIAN REPUBLIC, OVERWHELMINGLY BEATING GORBACHEV'S PREFERRED CANDIDATE.

IN AUGUST 1991, DURING A BRIEF COUP AGAINST GORBACHEV BY HARD-LINE COMMUNISTS, YELTSIN DEFIED THE COUP LEADERS AND RALLIED RESISTANCE IN MOSCOW IN SUPPORT OF GORBACHEV. WHEN THE COUP CRUMBLED A FEW DAYS AFTER IT HAD BEGUN, YELTSIN EMERGED AS THE COUNTRY'S MOST POWERFUL POLITICAL FIGURE.

IMAGES OF YELTSIN STANDING ON A TANK OUTSIDE THE PARLIAMENT IN MOSCOW DURING THE COUP BROUGHT HIM TO WORLD PROMINENCE.

THE RUSSIAN GOVERNMENT UNDER YELTSIN THEN ASSUMED THE FUNCTIONS OF THE COLLAPSING SOVIET GOVERNMENT. THE VARIOUS REPUBLICS AGREED TO FORM A NEW COMMONWEALTH AND ON 25 DECEMBER 1991, GORBACHEV RESIGNED THE PRESIDENCY OF THE SOVIET UNION, WHICH CEASED TO EXIST THE SAME DAY.

BY THIS TIME, ANATOLY SOBCHAK HAD BEEN ELECTED MAYOR OF LENINGRAD, VLADIMIR PUTIN HAD BECOME ADVISOR ON INTERNATIONAL RELATIONS, AND, IN A REFERENDUM, LENINGRAD'S CITIZENS HAD VOTED FOR THE NAME OF THEIR CITY TO BE CHANGED BACK TO ITS PRE-SOVIET NAME OF ST PETERSBURG.

ONCE THE POLITICAL SITUATION HAD BEGUN TO STABILISE, MARINA SALYE CONTINUED HER INVESTIGATION INTO THE 90 MILLION DEUTSCHMARKS WORTH OF MISSING MEAT.

SHE DISCOVERED THAT THE NAME OF THE MAN WHO HAD NEGOTIATED THIS DEAL WAS VLADIMIR PUTIN.

PUTIN'S DEPARTMENT IN THE MAYOR'S OFFICE WAS CALLED THE COMMITTEE FOR FOREIGN RELATIONS.

MOST OF ITS ACTIVITY CENTRED ON PROVIDING FOOD TO BE BROUGHT INTO THE CITY FROM OTHER COUNTRIES.

SALYE FOUND THAT PUTIN'S DEPARTMENT HAD ENTERED INTO MULTIPLE EXPORT CONTRACTS OF QUESTIONABLE LEGALITY.

AT THIS TIME RUSSIA'S CURRENCY, THE ROUBLE, WAS WORTH VERY LITTLE, BUT THE COUNTRY DID HAVE PLENTY OF NATURAL RESOURCES IT COULD TRADE: OIL, METALS, TIMBER, COTTON, ETC.

THE COMPANIES NAMED ON THESE CONTRACTS UNDERTOOK TO EXPORT THE NATURAL RESOURCES AND IMPORT FOODSTUFFS.

BUT SALYE DISCOVERED THAT EVERY ONE OF THESE CONTRACTS CONTAINED A FLAW THAT MADE IT INVALID. OFTEN THE CONTRACTS WERE MISSING SEALS OR SIGNATURES.

SALYE KNEW THAT PUTIN WAS A TRAINED LAWYER WHO MUST HAVE BEEN AWARE THAT THESE CONTRACTS WOULD NOT HOLD UP IN COURT.

THE COMMODITIES MENTIONED WERE APPARENTLY EXPORTED, BUT THE FOOD NEVER APPEARED.

THE FRAUD OPERATED THROUGH THE CREATION OF A LEGALLY FLAWED CONTRACT WITH SOMEONE WHO WOULD RUBBER STAMP AN EXPORT LICENCE...

...SO THAT THE CUSTOMS OFFICE WOULD OPEN THE BORDER, THE GOODS COULD BE SHIPPED ABROAD, SOLD, AND THE MONEY POCKETED.

MOSCOW HAD GIVEN ST PETERSBURG PERMISSION TO EXPORT A BILLION DOLLARS' WORTH OF COMMODITIES, SO THE TWELVE RIGGED CONTRACTS SALYE FOUND REPRESENTED ONLY A TENTH OF THE WEALTH THAT SHOULD HAVE MOVED THROUGH PUTIN'S OFFICE.

SALYE HAD PROOF THAT $92 MILLION HAD VANISHED AND SHE HAD SUSPICIONS ABOUT ANOTHER $900 MILLION OF CITY MONEY.

AFTER REVIEWING THE EVIDENCE THE CITY COUNCIL CONCLUDED THAT THE MONEY HAD BEEN STOLEN.

THEY URGED MAYOR SOBCHAK TO DISMISS PUTIN AND HIS DEPUTY, ALEKSANDER ANIKIN.

BUT INSTEAD OF TAKING ACTION AGAINST THE CORRUPTION, SOBCHAK ABOLISHED THE CITY COUNCIL.

GO!

IN THE EARLY '90s A FEW PEOPLE IN RUSSIA GOT RICH VERY FAST. COLOSSAL LEVELS OF CORRUPTION WERE WIDESPREAD.

BUT FOR ORDINARY PEOPLE THE BENEFITS OF A POST-SOVIET RUSSIA NEVER APPEARED.

THERE'S LOTS OF GOODS IN THE STORES NOW.

WHICH WE CAN'T AFFORD.

IN ST PETERSBURG THREE QUARTERS OF THE POPULATION LIVED BELOW THE POVERTY LINE.

POVERTY LINE

THE CITY'S INFRASTRUCTURE WAS CRUMBLING. PUBLIC TRANSPORT WAS AT A STANDSTILL.

WHEN IS THE BUS DUE?

IT ISN'T.

BUS STOP

IN A CITY OF LARGE APARTMENT BUILDINGS, WORKING LIFTS WERE RARE.

LIFT

OUT OF ORDER

HOWEVER, MAYOR SOBCHAK LIVED A RICH CELEBRITY LIFESTYLE, SEEMINGLY OBLIVIOUS TO THE CITY'S DECLINE...

29

...AND THE FACT THAT HE WAS HUGELY UNPOPULAR WITH VOTERS. HE LOST THE 1996 MAYORAL ELECTION TO HIS FORMER FIRST DEPUTY VLADIMIR YAKOVLEV.

WHAT?

PUTIN, PROMOTED TO SOBCHAK'S DEPUTY IN '94, TURNED DOWN A JOB IN THE NEW CITY ADMINISTRATION. INSTEAD, HE TOOK HIS FAMILY AND MOVED TO MOSCOW...

...WHERE HE BECAME DEPUTY HEAD OF THE PRESIDENTIAL PROPERTY MANAGEMENT DEPARTMENT. IT WAS ANOTHER PLUM JOB MYSTERIOUSLY FOUND.

MEANWHILE, SOBCHAK HAD LOST NOT ONLY THE ELECTION BUT ALSO IMMUNITY FROM PROSECUTION.

THE LAW

A TEAM OF NEARLY 40 SPECIAL INVESTIGATORS SPENT A YEAR LOOKING AT ALLEGATIONS OF CORRUPTION IN THE MAYOR'S OFFICE.

THE LAW

ON THE DAY SOBCHAK PRESENTED HIMSELF AT THE PROSECUTOR'S OFFICE, HE HAD A HEART ATTACK.

AFTER RECOVERING, SOBCHAK TRAVELLED TO FRANCE FOR FURTHER MEDICAL TREATMENT.

AIRPORT OFFICIALS STATED THAT HE SEEMED PHYSICALLY WELL WHEN HE BOARDED THE PLANE — ALMOST RUNNING FROM THE AMBULANCE.

SOBCHAK DID NOT RETURN TO RUSSIA UNTIL 1999. HE REMAINED IN SELF-IMPOSED EXILE IN PARIS, WELL OUT OF REACH OF RUSSIAN INVESTIGATORS.

DURING THOSE YEARS, HIS FORMER DEPUTY, VLADIMIR PUTIN, ROSE UPWARDS THROUGH THE RANKS OF POWER, SEEMINGLY WITHOUT EFFORT.

WHAT INFLUENCE PUTIN'S FORMER MASTERS IN THE KGB HAD ON HIS RISE IS UNKNOWN, BUT IT IS HARD TO BELIEVE THEIR INVISIBLE HAND WAS NOT INVOLVED.

BY 1998, PUTIN HAD BEEN MADE FIRST DEPUTY HEAD OF THE PRESIDENTIAL ADMINISTRATION.

BORIS YELTSIN'S LEADERSHIP OF THE RUSSIAN FEDERATION WAS OFTEN ERRATIC AND CRUDE. HE WAS NEVER RELUCTANT TO USE THE PRESIDENCY TO FACE DOWN HIS OPPONENTS — AS HE DID IN 1993, WHEN HE ORDERED TANKS TO FIRE ON A RUSSIAN PARLIAMENT DOMINATED BY OPENLY SEDITIOUS COMMUNISTS (AN UNCONSTITUTIONAL ACT TO DISSOLVE CONGRESS, WHICH LED TO NEW PARLIAMENTARY ELECTIONS) AND AGAIN IN 1994, WHEN HE EMBARKED ON A MILITARY OPERATION TO CRUSH THE BREAKAWAY REPUBLIC OF CHECHNYA.

BUT HE ENSURED THAT THERE WOULD BE NO RETURNING TO THE CENTRALISED SOVIET COMMAND ECONOMY, WHICH HAD STRANGLED GROWTH AND REDUCED THE COUNTRY TO PENURY. HOWEVER, HIS ECONOMIC PLANS DID NOT ALWAYS BRING ABOUT THE DESIRED RESULTS.

IN 1992, YELTSIN LAUNCHED A PROGRAMME OF FREE VOUCHERS AS A WAY TO BOOST PRIVATISATION. UNDER THIS PROGRAMME, EVERY CITIZEN WAS ISSUED VOUCHERS (WORTH AROUND 10,000 ROUBLES), FOR THE PURCHASE OF SHARES OF SELECT STATE ENTERPRISES. WITHIN MONTHS, THE MAJORITY OF THEM WERE BOUGHT UP BY INSIDERS WHO OFFERED THE CITIZENS CASH.

ORDINARY RUSSIANS GOT NOTHING OUT OF THE VOUCHER PRIVATISATION. THE ONLY PEOPLE WHO BENEFITED WERE THE INSIDERS AND FINANCIAL OPERATORS WHO BOUGHT UP ALL THE VOUCHERS AND GAINED CONTROL OF THE MAIN ENTERPRISES AT A FRACTION OF THEIR MARKET VALUE.

IN 1995, IT HAPPENED AGAIN. YELTSIN WAS STRUGGLING TO FINANCE RUSSIA'S GROWING DEBT AND HE NEEDED TO WIN FAVOUR WITH BUSINESS LEADERS AHEAD OF THE 1996 ELECTION. TO AID THIS EFFORT, HE PREPARED FOR A NEW WAVE OF PRIVATISATION, OFFERING STOCK SHARES IN SOME OF RUSSIA'S MOST VALUABLE STATE ENTERPRISES IN EXCHANGE FOR BANK LOANS TO FINANCE HIS RE-ELECTION CAMPAIGN.

HOWEVER, THESE DEALS WERE EFFECTIVELY GIVEAWAYS OF THE STATE'S ASSETS TO A SMALL GROUP OF TYCOONS IN FINANCE, INDUSTRY, ENERGY AND TELECOMMUNICATIONS, CREATING A CLASS OF SUPER-RICH INDIVIDUALS WHO CAME TO BE KNOWN AS OLIGARCHS, AND WHO THEN PLUNDERED THE RESOURCES OF THE COUNTRY.

BORIS YELTSIN WAS RE-ELECTED TO THE PRESIDENCY IN 1996.

HIS SECOND TERM WAS DOMINATED BY THE CHECHEN WAR, HIS HEALTH ISSUES, AN ATTEMPT TO IMPEACH HIM (WHICH FAILED), AND HIS ERRATIC BEHAVIOUR CAUSED BY ALCOHOLISM.

IN NOVEMBER 1996, HE UNDERWENT EMERGENCY QUINTUPLE HEART SURGERY AND WAS IN HOSPITAL FOR MONTHS.

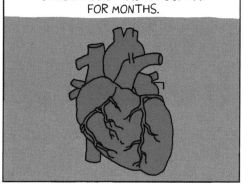

RUSSIAN DOMESTIC POLITICS REMAINED CHAOTIC. YELTSIN DISMISSED FOUR PRIME MINISTERS IN THIS PERIOD.

AND, IN 1998, HE FIRED HIS ENTIRE CABINET...

GET LOST!

...ALTHOUGH MANY WERE REAPPOINTED.

COME BACK!

AS THE YEARS WENT ON, YELTSIN WAS SEEN AS AN INCREASINGLY DRUNK AND UNSTABLE LEADER.

IN HIS AUTOBIOGRAPHY, *MIDNIGHT DIARIES*, YELTSIN STATES HOW HE USED ALCOHOL AS AN EASY WAY OF DE-STRESSING.

GONE WAS THE INSPIRING POLITICIAN, REPLACED BY A STUMBLING AND EMBARRASSING CARICATURE.

YELTSIN NEEDED A SUCCESSOR, SOMEONE WHO COULD ENSURE HE WOULD NOT FACE CORRUPTION CHARGES ONCE HE LEFT OFFICE.

HE LOOKED AROUND AND SAW VLADIMIR PUTIN.

YELTSIN REMEMBERED THAT PUTIN WAS DIFFERENT FROM OTHER DEPUTIES. HE DID NOT TRY AND LAY OUT HIS VISION OF RUSSIA AND THE WORLD. HE MADE NO EFFORT TO STRIKE UP CONVERSATION WITH YELTSIN, AND BECAUSE OF THIS, YELSIN FOUND THAT HE WANTED TO TALK TO HIM MORE.

BY 1998, PUTIN WAS DIRECTOR OF THE FEDERAL SECURITY SERVICE (FSB) — THE SUCCESSOR TO THE KGB.

IN 1999, YELTSIN APPOINTED HIM PRIME MINISTER.

YELTSIN ANNOUNCED HIS RESIGNATION THAT DECEMBER LIVE ON TELEVISION.

HE NAMED PRIME MINISTER VLADIMIR PUTIN ACTING PRESIDENT

ANGERED BY PUTIN'S CANDIDACY FOR THE PRESIDENCY, MARINA SALYE SPOKE OUT.

SHE WROTE AN ELOQUENTLY INSIGHTFUL ATTACK ON PUTIN, ACCUSING HIM OF·CORRUPTION AND OLIGARCHIC PRACTICES.

BUT SHE FOUND HERSELF MARGINALISED. DURING A MEETING OF THE RIGHT–LIBERAL COALITION, SHE AND YELTSIN'S FIRST PRIME MINISTER, YEGOR GAIDAR, WERE THE ONLY PEOPLE OUT OF OVER A HUNDRED WHO DIDN'T VOTE IN FAVOUR OF PUTIN.

SALYE ATTEMPTED TO FORM AN ALLIANCE WITH ANOTHER LIBERAL RUSSIAN POLITICIAN, SERGEI YUSHENKOV, WELL KNOWN FOR HIS CAMPAIGNS FOR DEMOCRACY, FREE MARKET ECONOMIC REFORMS AND HUMAN RIGHTS.

IN A VISIT TO YUSHENKOV'S OFFICE, SHE FOUND ANOTHER MAN THERE, WHO EVEN YEARS LATER SHE WOULD NOT IDENTIFY.

SALYE DIDN'T KNOW WHAT THE MAN WAS DOING THERE OR WHY YUSHENKOV SIMPLY DIDN'T ASK HIM TO LEAVE THE OFFICE WHEN SHE ARRIVED.

SHE CONCLUDED THAT THIS MEANT THAT HE WAS UNABLE TO GET RID OF HIM, EVEN THOUGH THE CONVERSATION THAT SHE AND YUSHENKOV WERE ABOUT TO HAVE WAS PRIVATE.

WHATEVER THIS UNKNOWN MAN SAID TO SALYE SCARED HER SO MUCH THAT SHE WENT INTO HIDING. SHE MOVED TO A REMOTE VILLAGE AND DID NOT SPEAK TO JOURNALISTS FOR TEN YEARS.

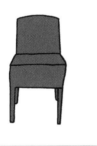

SERGEI YUSHENKOV LEFT THE LIBERAL FACTION OF PARLIAMENT IN PROTEST AGAINST HIS COLLEAGUES' SUPPORT FOR PUTIN.

ON 17 APRIL 2003, WHILE WALKING TO HIS APARTMENT BUILDING IN NORTHERN MOSCOW...

...HE WAS SHOT IN THE CHEST MULTIPLE TIMES.

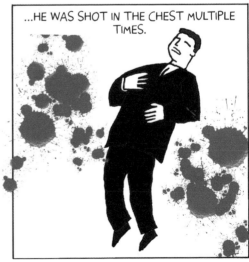

BUT WHAT OF ANATOLY SOBCHAK, PUTIN'S MENTOR AND THE EX-MAYOR OF ST PETERSBURG?

IN THE SUMMER OF 1999, ENCOURAGED BY THE RISE TO POWER OF HIS FORMER DEPUTY, AND NO DOUBT SEEING HIMSELF NOW PROTECTED FROM PROSECUTION...

...SOBCHAK ENDED HIS PARIS EXILE AND RETURNED TO RUSSIA. WHERE PUTIN APPOINTED HIS OLD BOSS AS AN 'EMPOWERED REPRESENTATIVE.'

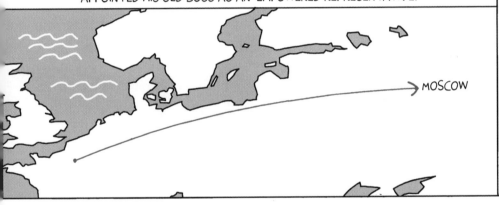

MOSCOW

HIS JOB WAS TO TRAVEL THE COUNTRY AND CAMPAIGN FOR PUTIN'S ELECTION. THIS IS WHERE SOBCHAK MAY HAVE EARNED PUTIN'S OR HIS ASSOCIATES' DISPLEASURE.

IN A NEWSPAPER ARTICLE HE WAS CRITICAL OF HOW THE KGB AND OTHER LAW ENFORCEMENT AGENCIES IN ST PETERSBURG HAD TAKEN OVER THE SEA PORT, SAYING THAT THOSE BEHIND IT SHOULD BE JAILED.

IN FEBRUARY 2000, PUTIN ASKED SOBCHAK TO CAMPAIGN FOR HIM IN KALININGRAD. THE FORMER MAYOR TRAVELLED THERE WITH TWO ASSISTANTS WHO DOUBLED AS BODYGUARDS.

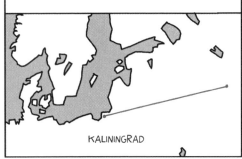

ON 20 FEBRUARY, SOBCHAK DIED AT A HOTEL IN A RESORT TOWN OUTSIDE KALININGRAD. THE OFFICIAL CAUSE OF DEATH WAS A HEART ATTACK.

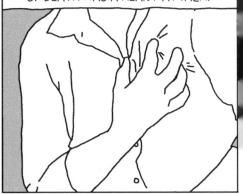

NONETHELESS, THE PROSECUTOR'S OFFICE IN KALININGRAD OPENED AN INVESTIGATION INTO A POSSIBLE CASE OF MURDER. THIS INVESTIGATION WAS SOON CLOSED WITHOUT A FINDING.

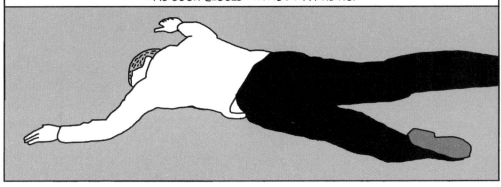

ARKADY VAKSBERG, A FORENSICS SPECIALIST TURNED INVESTIGATIVE REPORTER, LOOKED INTO THE CASE. HE DISCOVERED A PUZZLING DETAIL.

SOBCHAK'S BODYGUARDS — TWO HEALTHY YOUNG MEN — HAD TO BE TREATED FOR MILD POISONING FOLLOWING HIS DEATH.

THIS INDICATED TO VAKSBERG THAT SOBCHAK'S DEATH WAS NOT NATURAL, BUT A CONTRACT KILLING. IN SUCH CASES IT WAS NOT UNUSUAL FOR A SECRETARY OR BODYGUARD TO FALL ILL TOO WHEN THEIR BOSSES WERE KILLED. IN 2007, VAKSBERG PUBLISHED A BOOK ON THE HISTORY OF POLITICAL POISONINGS IN THE USSR AND RUSSIA, CALLED *TOXIC POLITICS*.

IN THE BOOK, HE ADVANCED THE THEORY THAT SOBCHAK WAS KILLED WITH A POISON PLACED ON THE BULB OF A BEDSIDE LAMP, SO THAT WHEN THE LAMP WAS TURNED ON THE SUBSTANCE WAS HEATED AND VAPORISED.

A FEW MONTHS AFTER THE BOOK WAS PUBLISHED, VAKSBERG'S CAR WAS BLOWN UP. FORTUNATELY, HE WAS NOT IN IT.

ON 22 SEPTEMBER, A SUSPICIOUS DEVICE RESEMBLING THOSE USED IN THESE BOMBINGS WAS FOUND AND DEFUSED IN AN APARTMENT BLOCK IN THE RUSSIAN CITY OF RYAZAN.

THE NEXT DAY, THE ACTING PRESIDENT VLADIMIR PUTIN PRAISED THE VIGILANCE OF THE INHABITANTS OF RYAZAN AND ORDERED THE AIR BOMBING OF THE CHECHEN CITY OF GROZNY.

BUT ALL WAS NOT AS IT APPEARED. THE TWO MEN AND ONE WOMAN WHO HAD PLACED THE BOMBS IN RYAZAN TURNED OUT TO BE NOT CHECHEN TERRORISTS, BUT AGENTS OF THE FSB, ONE OF THE SUCCESSOR AGENCIES OF THE SOVIET-ERA KGB. AFTER THESE AGENTS WERE ARRESTED BY LOCAL POLICE, NIKOLAI PATRUSHEV, THE HEAD OF THE FSB, SAID THAT THE BOMB HAD BEEN A FAKE AND THAT IT HAD BEEN PLANTED IN RYAZAN AS PART OF A TRAINING EXERCISE.

HOWEVER, THE BOMB HAD TESTED POSITIVE FOR HEXOGEN RDX, THE SAME EXPLOSIVE USED IN THE FOUR APARTMENT BOMBINGS. THESE SUSPICIOUS EVENTS LED TO ALLEGATIONS THAT THE BOMBINGS WERE IN FACT A 'FALSE FLAG' ATTACK PERPETRATED BY THE FSB IN ORDER TO LEGITIMISE THE RESUMPTION OF MILITARY ACTIVITIES IN CHECHNYA AND BRING VLADIMIR PUTIN AND THE FSB TO POWER.

VLADIMIR PUTIN WAS INAUGURATED AS PRESIDENT ON 7 MAY 2000.

HIS ADMINISTRATION BEGAN ROLLING BACK THE COUNTRY'S DEMOCRATIC REFORMS ALMOST AT ONCE.

FOUR DAYS AFTER THE INAUGURATION, ARMED POLICE RAIDED THE OFFICES OF VLADIMIR GUSINSKY, THE TYCOON WHO OWNED THE MEDIA-MOST EMPIRE...

...WHICH INCLUDED THE TV CHANNEL NTV...

...PUTIN'S MOST VOCAL CRITIC.

CLICK!

...V'S WEEKLY SATIRICAL SHOW *KUKLY*, OR *PUPPETS* (INSPIRED BY THE 1980s–90s BRITISH SHOW *SPITTING IMAGE*, WHICH USED PUPPETS TO REPRESENT CELEBRITIES), PORTRAYED PUTIN AS AN UNGAINLY DWARF FROM AN ETA HOFFMANN FAIRY TALE, WHO INHERITED A READY-MADE KINGDOM OF GREAT RICHES THROUGH NO EFFORT OF HIS OWN. NTV HAD ALSO ANGERED THE KREMLIN BY LAUNCHING AN IN-DEPTH INVESTIGATION INTO THE POSSIBILITY THAT THE FSB HAD STAGED THE APARTMENT BLOCK EXPLOSIONS IN ORDER TO INFLUENCE THE ELECTION.

AS A RESULT THE OWNER, VLADIMIR GUSINSKY, WAS JAILED ON POSSIBLY TRUMPED-UP EMBEZZLEMENT CHARGES...

...AND ULTIMATELY HAD TO FLEE THE COUNTRY, AFTER RELINQUISHING CONTROL OF ALL HIS MEDIA HOLDINGS.

TEN DAYS AFTER THE INAUGURATION, PUTIN UNVEILED NEW PLANS TO REIN IN THE POWERS OF RUSSIA'S REGIONAL GOVERNORS — MEASURES INTENDED TO ENSURE THAT THE ELECTED GOVERNORS COULD NEVER UNITE AGAINST THE KREMLIN.

THE PROPOSED LEGISLATION WOULD TAKE AWAY THE GOVERNORS' SEATS IN THE FEDERATION COUNCIL, THE UPPER CHAMBER OF PARLIAMENT, WHICH ALSO REMOVED THEIR IMMUNITY FROM PROSECUTION.

THIS EFFORT TO CENTRALISE POWER BROUGHT PUTIN AND HIS ADMINISTRATION INTO CONFLICT WITH ONE OF THE MOST POWERFUL RUSSIAN OLIGARCHS – BORIS BEREZOVSKY.

BEREZOVSKY HAD MADE HIS FORTUNE IN RUSSIA IN THE 1990s DURING THE PRIVATISATION OF STATE PROPERTY. HE PROFITED FROM GAINING CONTROL OVER VARIOUS ASSETS, INCLUDING THE COUNTRY'S MAIN TELEVISION CHANNEL, CHANNEL ORT. IN 1997, FORBES ESTIMATED BEREZOVSKY'S WEALTH AT $3 BILLION.

BEREZOVSKY ATTACKED THE CONSTITUTIONAL REFORM PROPOSED BY THE PRESIDENT. AN OPEN LETTER TO PUTIN, PUBLISHED IN THE DAILY NEWSPAPER *KOMMERSANT*, BEREZOVSKY, WHO WAS ALSO A DEPUTY IN THE DUMA (PART OF THE RUSSIAN PARLIAMENT), SAID THAT HE WOULD VOTE AGAINST THE PRESIDENT'S LEGISLATIVE PROJECT.

HE BELIEVED THE LEGISLATION WAS AIMED AT CHANGING THE STRUCTURE OF THE STATE AND WAS A THREAT TO RUSSIA'S TERRITORIAL INTEGRITY AND DEMOCRACY.

ON 17 JULY 2000, BEREZOVSKY RESIGNED FROM THE DUMA...

...REFUSING TO INVOLVE HIMSELF IN THE RESTORATION OF A DICTATORSHIP IN RUSSIA.

THEN CAME THE KURSK DISASTER. THE FIRST REAL CRISIS OF THE PUTIN ADMINISTRATION.

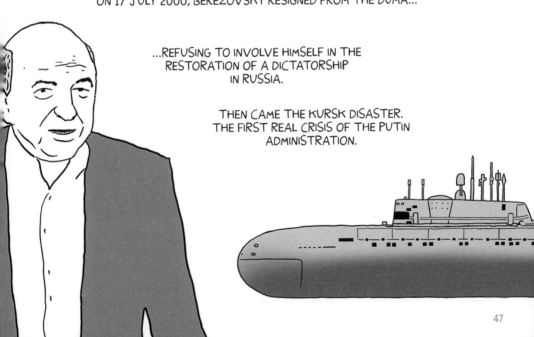

THE NUCLEAR-POWERED OSCAR II CLASS SUBMARINE, KURSK, SANK IN AN ACCIDENT ON 12 AUGUST 2000 IN THE BARENTS SEA. THIS WAS THE FIRST MAJOR RUSSIAN NAVAL EXERCISE IN MORE THAN TEN YEARS. MOST OF THE 118 CREW DIED INSTANTLY.

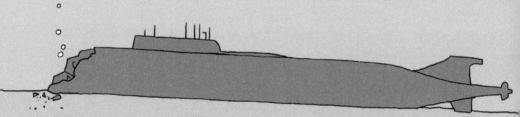

TWENTY-THREE SURVIVORS MOVED TO AN UNAFFECTED SECTION OF THE VESSEL TO AWAIT RESCUE. NORWEGIAN AND BRITISH TEAMS OFFERED TO HELP BUT WERE TURNED AWAY, BECAUSE THE RUSSIANS FEARED DISCLOSURE ABOUT THE STATE OF ITS NUCLEAR FLEET.

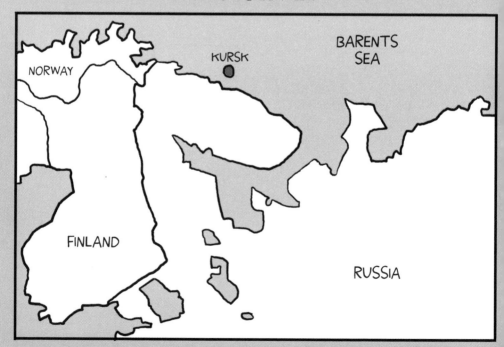

THE KURSK HAD GONE TO SEA WITH AN UNPRACTICED AND UNDERTRAINED CREW, DRAWN FROM SEVERAL DIFFERENT SHIPS. THE SUBMARINE WAS EQUIPPED WITH TRAINING TORPEDOES, SOME OF WHICH WERE PAST THEIR EXPIRATION DATES, WHILE THE REST HAD NOT BEEN PROPERLY SERVICED. IT WAS ONE OF THESE TORPEDOES THAT CAUGHT FIRE AND EXPLODED.

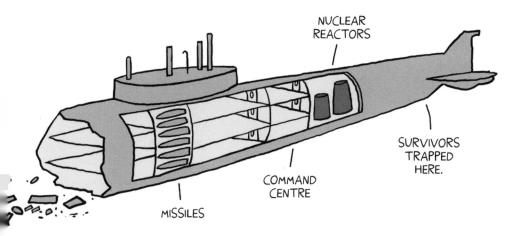

NUCLEAR REACTORS

SURVIVORS TRAPPED HERE.

COMMAND CENTRE

MISSILES

OVER FOUR DAYS, THE RUSSIAN NAVY REPEATEDLY FAILED TO ATTACH FOUR DIFFERENT DIVING BELLS AND SUBMERSIBLES TO THE ESCAPE HATCH OF THE SUBMARINE. FINALLY, TEN DAYS AFTER THE SINKING, BRITISH AND NORWEGIAN DIVERS WERE GIVEN PERMISSION BY PUTIN TO ENTER THE SUB. THEY FOUND NO SURVIVORS IN THE BOAT'S FLOODED NINTH COMPARTMENT. THEY WERE TOO LATE.

WHERE WAS PUTIN WHILE ALL THIS WAS HAPPENING? HE WAS AT HIS SUMMER RESIDENCE NEAR SOCHI, ON THE BLACK SEA COAST, ONLY APPEARING — IN FOOTAGE SHOWN BY BEREZOVSKY'S CHANNEL ORT — ON A JETSKI, TANNED AND RELAXED IN LIGHT-COLOURED RESORT CLOTHING. PUTIN STAYED SILENT, WHILE THE NAVY WERE EVASIVE OVER EXACTLY WHAT HAD HAPPENED, EVEN AFTER ACKNOWLEDGING THAT THE SUBMARINE HAD SUNK.

PUTIN DID NOT FLY BACK TO MOSCOW UNTIL SEVEN DAYS AFTER THE DISASTER.

EVEN THEN, HE DID NOT APPEAR IN PUBLIC FOR ANOTHER THREE DAYS...

...WHEN HE TRAVELLED TO VIDYAYEVO, A MILITARY CITY ABOVE THE ARCTIC CIRCLE, AND THE KURSK'S HOME PORT.

HERE, HE SPOKE FOR MORE THAN TWO HOURS TO ANGRY AND GRIEVING FAMILY MEMBERS OF THE KURSK DEAD. THEY DID NOT PULL THEIR PUNCHES.

WHY DID YOU TAKE SO LONG IN GETTING FOREIGN HELP?

HE CAME OUT OF THAT MEETING, STUNNED AND DISTURBED, DECIDING NEVER AGAIN TO MEET THE PUBLIC IN SUCH CIRCUMSTANCES.

HE HAD DUCKED RESPONSIBILITY BY BLAMING THE BUNGLED RESCUE OPERATION ON THE PITIFUL STATE OF THE NAVY, WHICH FOR YEARS HAD BEEN LEFT TO DECAY WITH LITTLE FUNDING.

PUTIN WAS FURIOUS ABOUT HOW HE'D BEEN PORTRAYED IN THE MEDIA. HE VOWED TO CRACK DOWN ON OLIGARCHS AND LIMIT THEIR POLITICAL POWER.

HE MADE THE CLAIM THAT THERE WERE INDIVIDUALS ON TELEVISION WHO FOR TEN YEARS HAD BEEN WORKING TO DESTROY RUSSIA'S ARMED FORCES. THEY PRETENDED TO DEFEND THE MILITARY WHEN, IN FACT, THEY REALLY WANTED TO DESTROY IT. THESE PEOPLE HAD STOLEN BILLIONS IN MONEY AND HAD USED IT TO BUY POLITICIANS AND MAKE LAWS THAT BENEFITED THEM.

IN MID-OCTOBER, PROSECUTORS REOPENED THEIR CASE INTO ALLEGATIONS THAT BEREZOVSKY HAD SIPHONED HUNDREDS OF MILLIONS OF DOLLARS THROUGH SWISS COMPANIES FROM AEROFLOT, THE RUSSIAN STATE AIRLINE HE PART-OWNED.

BEREZOVSKY IMMEDIATELY FLED RUSSIA, JOINING GUSINSKY IN EXILE.

HE COMPLAINED THAT PUTIN AND HIS ALLIES HAD FORCED HIM TO CHOOSE BETWEEN BEING A POLITICAL PRISONER OR A POLITICAL ÉMIGRÉ.

BEREZOVSKY THEN SOLD HIS SHARES IN CHANNEL ORT TO FELLOW OLIGARCH ROMAN ABRAMOVICH, WHO PROMPTLY SOLD THE SHARES TO THE STATE.

LESS THAN A YEAR AFTER PUTIN CAME TO POWER, ALL THREE FEDERAL NETWORKS WERE CONTROLLED BY THE STATE.

ON 23 OCTOBER 2002 THERE WAS A TERRORIST ATTACK IN RUSSIA.

AT LEAST 40 ARMED CHECHEN FIGHTERS WALKED INTO THE DUBROVKA MUSICAL THEATRE IN MOSCOW (ONLY THREE AND A HALF MILES FROM THE KREMLIN), FIRING ASSAULT RIFLES INTO THE AIR JUST AS TAPDANCERS TROUPED ACROSS THE STAGE FOR THE OPENING OF THE SECOND ACT OF A POPULAR NEW RUSSIAN MUSICAL, *NORD-OST*. NINE HUNDRED AND TWELVE PEOPLE WERE TAKEN HOSTAGE.

THE CHECHENS, LED BY MOVSAR BARAYEV, THE NEPHEW OF ONE OF CHECHNYA'S MOST RENOWNED REBELS, WERE DEMANDING AN END TO RUSSIA'S WAR IN THE REPUBLIC, WHICH HAD BEEN GOING ON EVER SINCE THE 1999 APARTMENT BLOCK BOMBINGS.

THE CHECHENS WIRED THE BUILDING WITH EXPLOSIVES.

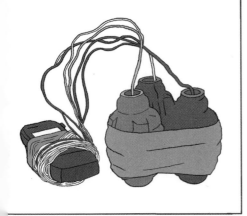

WOMEN KNOWN AS 'BLACK WIDOWS' WHO APPEARED TO HAVE EXPLOSIVES STRAPPED TO THEIR BODIES...

...STATIONED THEMSELVES AMONG THE HOSTAGES.

WE ARE FOLLOWING ALLAH'S PATH. IF WE DIE HERE, THAT WON'T BE THE END OF IT.

IN THE EARLY HOURS OF THE MORNING, ON 24 OCTOBER, OLGA ROMANOVA, A 26-YEAR-OLD PERFUME SHOP CLERK, SOMEHOW AVOIDED THE POLICE CORDON AND ENTERED THE THEATRE...

...WHERE, ACCORDING TO DIFFERING ACCOUNTS, SHE EITHER TRIED TO NEGOTIATE WITH THE TERRORISTS OR URGED THE HOSTAGES TO FIGHT THEIR CAPTORS.

SHE WAS THEN SHOT DEAD.

THE SIEGE WENT ON FOR THREE DAYS. THE SECURITY SERVICES FINALLY ACTED JUST BEFORE DAWN ON SATURDAY 26 OCTOBER.

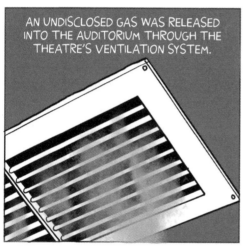

AN UNDISCLOSED GAS WAS RELEASED INTO THE AUDITORIUM THROUGH THE THEATRE'S VENTILATION SYSTEM.

THE DISCOVERY OF THE GAS CAUSED PANIC. HOSTAGE ANNA ANDRIANOVA, A REPORTER FOR *MOSKOVSKAYA PRAVDA*, CALLED ECHO OF MOSCOW RADIO STUDIO...

AND IN A LIVE BROADCAST INTERVIEW SHE SAID...

PLEASE, GIVE US A CHANCE. IF YOU CAN DO ANYTHING, PLEASE DO! ... I DON'T KNOW WHICH GAS IT IS. BUT I SEE [THE CHECHENS'] REACTIONS.

WE SEE IT, WE FEEL IT, WE ARE BREATHING THROUGH OUR CLOTHES... ... IT BEGAN FROM OUTSIDE. THAT'S WHAT OUR GOVERNMENT HAS DECIDED – THAT NO ONE SHOULD LEAVE HERE ALIVE.

THE GAS USED IS BELIEVED TO HAVE BEEN A DERIVATIVE OF THE ANAESTHETIC FENTANYL, A POTENT OPIOID WIDELY USED AS A PAINKILLER.

THE AIM WAS TO RENDER THE TERRORISTS UNCONSCIOUS SO THAT THE HOSTAGES COULD BE FREED, BUT THE PLAN WENT DISASTROUSLY WRONG.

BECAUSE THE GAS KNOCKED OUT THE HOSTAGES AND ONLY SOME OF THE INSURGENTS.

THIRTY MINUTES AFTER THE GAS WAS RELEASED A PHYSICAL ASSAULT OF THE BUILDING BEGAN.

IN A FIERCE FIREFIGHT THE SECURITY SERVICES KILLED THE TERRORISTS.

THOSE FOUND UNCONSCIOUS WERE SIMPLY SHOT WHERE THEY LAY.

THE UNCONSCIOUS HOSTAGES NEEDED MEDICAL HELP TO WAKE UP, WHICH THEY DID NOT GET.

THEY WERE SIMPLY CARRIED OUT OF THE BUILDING AND LAID ON THE STEPS OF THE THEATRE.

INSTEAD OF BEING PLACED ON THEIR SIDES IN THE RECOVERY POSITION THEY WERE LAID ON THEIR BACKS, SO THAT MANY CHOKED TO DEATH ON THEIR OWN VOMIT WITHOUT EVER REGAINING CONSCIOUSNESS. AFTER 90 MINUTES AMBULANCES ARRIVED, BUT THEY WERE NOT EQUIPPED TO DEAL WITH GAS CASUALTIES AND THE AUTHORITIES WOULD NOT TELL THEM WHAT TYPE OF GAS IT WAS.

THERE ARE DIFFERING REPORTS ON HOW MANY HOSTAGES DIED, BUT IT WAS AT LEAST 130. THE MAJORITY DIED FROM THE EFFECTS OF THE GAS.

IN THE AFTERMATH OF THE SIEGE, QUESTIONS OVER HOW A GROUP OF ARMED TERRORISTS GAINED ACCESS TO CENTRAL MOSCOW, AND ABOUT THE SECURITY SERVICES' INEPT RESPONSE WERE LARGELY IGNORED.

MOST PEOPLE WERE SIMPLY RELIEVED THAT THE DEATH TOLL HADN'T BEEN HIGHER.

PUTIN'S POPULARITY RATINGS SURGED. HE EASILY WON RE-ELECTION IN 2004.

RUSSIA RAMPED UP ITS MILITARY ACTION IN CHECHNYA.

AND PEACE TALKS WITH CHECHEN LEADER ASLAN MASKHADOV ENDED.

CHECHNYA WAS NOT THE ONLY FORMER SOVIET REPUBLIC OF WHICH RUSSIA WAS ATTEMPTING TO REGAIN CONTROL...

UKRAINE WAS THE THIRD-BIGGEST FORMER SOVIET REPUBLIC, AFTER RUSSIA ITSELF, AND KAZAKHSTAN. NEARLY 30 PER CENT OF ITS POPULATION SPOKE RUSSIAN AS THEIR NATIVE LANGUAGE.

IT WAS STRATEGICALLY IMPORTANT. 85 PER CENT OF RUSSIAN GAS EXPORTS TO EUROPE WERE SHIPPED THROUGH UKRAINE'S PIPELINE NETWORK...

...AND UKRAINE'S CRIMEAN PENINSULA ON THE BLACK SEA WAS STILL HOME TO A RUSSIAN NAVAL BASE.

BUT UKRAINE WAS DIVIDED. PART OF THE COUNTRY WAS LOOKING WEST WITH SOME UKRAINIAN POLITICIANS FAVOURING EVENTUAL EUROPEAN UNION MEMBERSHIP; AN OUTCOME PUTIN CONSIDERED UNACCEPTABLE.

JOIN US.

SURE.

HOLD IT RIGHT THERE.

ONE OF THESE TROUBLESOME WEST-LEANING UKRAINIAN POLITICIANS WAS VIKTOR YUSHCHENKO.

YUSHCHENKO WAS, FROM 1990 TO 1993, THE FIRST DEPUTY CHAIRMAN OF THE BOARD AT BANK UKRAINA. IN THIS POSITION HE OVERSAW THE INTRODUCTION OF THE NATIONAL CURRENCY, THE HRYVNYA, IN 1996.

IN 1999, YUSHCHENKO WAS APPOINTED PRIME MINISTER BY PRESIDENT LEONID KUCHMA. HE IS CREDITED, BY MANY ANALYSTS, WITH HELPING UKRAINE EMERGE FROM A LENGTHY ECONOMIC CRISIS.

YET IN 2001 KUCHMA ABRUPTLY DISMISSED YUSHCHENKO. IN RESPONSE, YUSHCHENKO — WHOSE POPULARITY HAD BEEN GROWING — FORMED THE WIDE-RANGING DEMOCRATIC COALITION 'OUR UKRAINE'...

...WHICH SUCCEEDED IN THE PARLIAMENTARY ELECTIONS LATER THAT YEAR, AND PROVIDED A PLATFORM FOR YUSHCHENKO TO CREDIBLY CHALLENGE THE PRESIDENCY.

WORRYINGLY FOR MOSCOW, YUSHCHENKO FAVOURED CLOSER INTEGRATION WITH WESTERN EUROPE, WHICH INCLUDED JOINING NATO.

VIKTOR YUSHCHENKO'S MAIN RIVAL FOR THE PRESIDENCY WAS ANOTHER VIKTOR, — VIKTOR YANUKOVYCH, THE NEW PRIME MINISTER — WHO WAS STRONGLY SUPPORTED BY PUTIN.

IN EARLY SEPTEMBER 2004, YUSHCHENKO HAD DINNER WITH THE HEAD OF THE UKRAINIAN SECURITY SERVICE (SBU), IHOR SMESHKO, AND HIS DEPUTY, VOLODYMYR SATSIUK.

THE NEXT DAY HE FELT ILL. TERRIBLE CYSTS BROKE OUT ON HIS FACE. DOCTORS IN AUSTRIA, WHERE HE FLEW FOR TREATMENT, CONCLUDED THAT HE'D BEEN POISONED WITH A HIGHLY TOXIC DIOXIN. THE CYSTS LEFT HIM DISFIGURED.

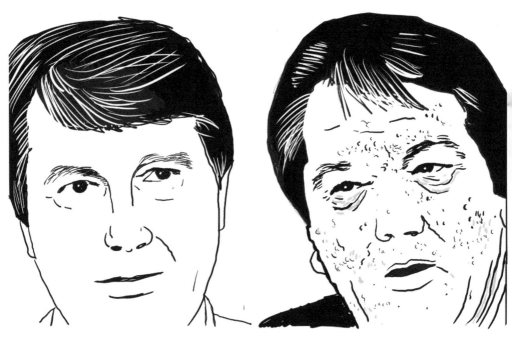

IN SEPTEMBER 2009, UKRAINIAN PROSECUTORS SAID THAT THEY HAD BEEN UNABLE TO OBTAIN TESTIMONY FOR AN INVESTIGATION FROM mR SATSIUK WHO HAD GONE TO MOSCOW AND HAD BEEN GIVEN RUSSIAN CITIZENSHIP WHICH PROTECTED HIM FROM EXTRADITION.

YUSHCHENKO SURVIVED THE POISONING AND WENT ON TO WIN A HIGHLY CONTESTED ELECTION, WHICH BECAME KNOWN AS THE ORANGE REVOLUTION.

IN THE SAME MONTH AS VIKTOR YUSHCHENKO'S POISONING IN 2004, THERE WAS ANOTHER BRUTAL TERROR ATTACK IN RUSSIA. THIS ONE TOOK PLACE IN THE SOUTHERN TOWN OF BESLAN.

THE FIRST DAY OF SCHOOL IN RUSSIA (THE DAY OF KNOWLEDGE) IS SOMETHING OF A HOLIDAY, AS STUDENTS ARRIVE IN THEIR BEST CLOTHES BEARING FLOWERS FOR THEIR TEACHERS.

AT APPROXIMATELY 9AM, AS THE CHILDREN OF BESLAN MILLED AROUND THE SCHOOL GATES FOR THE START-OF-SCHOOL CEREMONY, DOZENS OF ARMED TERRORISTS DROVE UP IN A POLICE TRUCK. THEY SEIZED THE SCHOOL, TAKING MORE THAN 1,100 PARENTS, CHILDREN AND TEACHERS HOSTAGE. SOME PEOPLE WERE MURDERED IN THE INITIAL ATTACK, THEIR BODIES THROWN FROM THE SCHOOL WINDOWS.

THE HOSTAGES WERE CRAMMED INTO A SMALL GYM. BOMBS WERE TAPED TO THE WALLS AND SUSPENDED FROM THE CEILING.

FOR TWO DAYS, THE HOSTAGES WERE REFUSED FOOD AND WATER DESPITE TERRIBLE HEAT. CHILDREN DRANK EACH OTHER'S URINE AND ATE THE FLOWERS THEY'D BROUGHT IN FOR THEIR TEACHERS.

PERIODICALLY THE ATTACKERS FIRED THEIR GUNS TO TERRIFY THE HOSTAGES AND PLACED CHILDREN ALONG THE WINDOWS TO ACT AS HUMAN SHIELDS.

RUSLAN AUSHEV, A VETERAN OF THE AFGHANISTAN WAR AND FORMER PRESIDENT OF THE NEIGHBOURING INGUSHETIA REGION...

...WENT INTO THE SCHOOL ALONE AND HELD TALKS WITH THE TERRORISTS. HE PROMPTLY SECURED THE RELEASE OF 26 MOTHERS AND BABIES...

...AND CARRIED OUT ONE OF THE CHILDREN HIMSELF.

THE SIEGE ENDED ON THE MORNING OF 3 SEPTEMBER, WHEN EXPLOSIONS INSIDE THE SCHOOL PROMPTED TROOPS, LED BY SPECIAL FORCES, TO STORM THE BUILDING.

AS THEY MOVED IN, HALF-NAKED AND BLOODIED CHILDREN BEGAN RUNNING OUT. OTHERS WERE CARRIED BY ADULTS. MANY HOSTAGES WERE KILLED BY EXPLOSIONS OR IN THE SUBSEQUENT FIRE IN THE GYM. OTHERS WERE MURDERED BY THE ATTACKERS, OR DIED IN THE CHAOS OF SHELLING AND GUNFIRE, CAUGHT IN THE CROSSFIRE.

63

EMERGENCY WORKERS, SIFTING THROUGH THE DEBRIS OF THE BURNT OUT GYMNASIUM, LATER
UNCOVERED THE REMAINS OF HUNDREDS OF CHILDREN AND ADULTS. THE SIEGE LEFT MORE THAN
330 PEOPLE DEAD, INCLUDING 186 CHILDREN.

MANY OF THE BODIES WERE CHARRED BEYOND RECOGNITION. SOME PARENTS HAD TO WAIT FOR
DNA TESTS TO CONFIRM THE FATE OF THEIR CHILDREN. MORE THAN 700 PEOPLE WERE INJURED.

TROOPS KILLED ALL BUT ONE OF A TOTAL OF 32 TERRORISTS.

QUESTIONS REMAINED. WHY DID THE RUSSIAN SPECIAL FORCES BEGIN ATTACKING THE BUILDING?

AND WHAT TRIGGERED THE FIRST EXPLOSION IN THE GYMNASIUM?

AN OFFICIAL KREMLIN INQUIRY CLEARED THE MILITARY OF ANY WRONGDOING.

BUT YURI SAVELYEV, AN INDEPENDENT DUMA DEPUTY AND WEAPONS AND EXPLOSIVES EXPERT...

...LED HIS OWN INVESTIGATION. HE FOUND THAT THE INITIAL EXPLOSION COULD ONLY HAVE BEEN CAUSED BY ROCKETS FIRED FROM OUTSIDE THE SCHOOL. HIS REPORT CONCLUDED THAT THE SPECIAL FORCES HAD FIRED ROCKET-PROPELLED GRENADES, WITHOUT WARNING, EVEN AS NEGOTIATIONS WERE GOING ON.

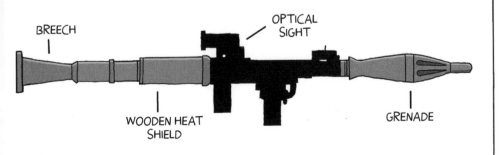

BREECH

OPTICAL SIGHT

WOODEN HEAT SHIELD

GRENADE

PUTIN USED THE BESLAN ATTACK TO FURTHER CONSOLIDATE HIS POWER.

TEN DAYS AFTER THE SIEGE HE ANNOUNCED THAT ELECTIONS FOR REGIONAL GOVERNORS WOULD BE ABOLISHED.

INSTEAD, GOVERNORS WOULD BE APPOINTED BY THE KREMLIN.

THE PRESIDENT CLAIMED THAT THIS MOVE WOULD STRENGTHEN THE SYSTEM AGAINST EXTERNAL THREATS.

PUTIN STATED THAT HE BELIEVED THAT TERRORISTS LIKE THE ONES WHO COMMITTED THE BESLAN ATROCITY WERE AIMING TO CAUSE THE DISINTEGRATION OF THE RUSSIAN STATE ITSELF, AND AS A RESULT, THE STATE NEEDED TO STRENGTHEN ITSELF TO WARD OFF FURTHER ATTACKS.

A JOURNALIST WHO INTENDED TO BE IN BESLAN COVERING THE SIEGE WAS ANNA POLITKOVSKAYA.

POLITKOVSKAYA, A REPORTER FOR THE INDEPENDENT BI-WEEKLY NEWSPAPER *NOVAYA GAZETA*, WAS AN OUTSPOKEN CRITIC OF PRESIDENT PUTIN AND THE RUSSIAN GOVERNMENT.

IT WAS HER REPORTING FROM CHECHNYA, ON THE MURDERS, TORTURE AND KIDNAPPING THAT TOOK PLACE ON BOTH SIDES OF THE CONFLICT, THAT MADE POLITKOVSKAYA'S NATIONAL AND INTERNATIONAL REPUTATION.

FOR YEARS SHE REFUSED TO GIVE UP REPORTING ON THE WAR DESPITE NUMEROUS ACTS OF INTIMIDATION AND VIOLENCE.

AS SOON AS NEWS BROKE OF THE SCHOOL SIEGE IN BESLAN, POLITKOVSKAYA ATTEMPTED TO TRAVEL TO NORTH OSSETIA. SHE REGISTERED FOR THREE CONSECUTIVE FLIGHTS, WHICH WERE ALL CANCELLED. SHE FINALLY GOT A SEAT ON A PLANE TO ROSTOV, THE LARGEST CITY IN SOUTHERN RUSSIA – STILL FOUR HUNDRED MILES FROM BESLAN. HER PLAN WAS TO HIRE A CAR AND DRIVE THE REST OF THE WAY. AS POLITKOVSKAYA HAD BEEN THE TARGET OF DEATH THREATS IN THE PAST, SHE DECIDED NOT TO EAT THE AIRPLANE FOOD...

AND ASKED ONLY FOR A CUP OF TEA. TEN MINUTES LATER, SHE LOST CONSCIOUSNESS.

SHE WAS STILL UNCONSCIOUS WHEN THE PLANE LANDED.

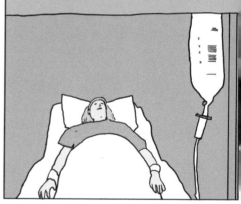

DOCTORS IN MOSCOW, WHERE SHE WAS TRANSPORTED TWO DAYS LATER, CONCLUDED SHE HAD BEEN POISONED...

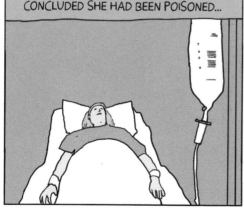

...WITH AN UNDISCLOSED TOXIN THAT DID SEVERE DAMAGE TO HER KIDNEYS, LIVER AND ENDOCRINE SYSTEM. IT TOOK MONTHS FOR HER TO RECOVER AND SHE NEVER ENTIRELY REGAINED HER HEALTH.

TWO YEARS LATER, ON SATURDAY 7 OCTOBER 2006, ANNA POLITKOVSKAYA WAS SHOT DEAD IN THE LIFT OF HER APARTMENT BUILDING IN CENTRAL MOSCOW: TWICE IN THE CHEST, ONCE IN THE SHOULDER AND ONCE IN THE HEAD AT POINT-BLANK RANGE.

PUTIN HAD TURNED 54 THAT DAY. MANY PEOPLE BELIEVED THAT THIS MURDER WAS A BIRTHDAY PRESENT.

BEFORE POLITKOVSKAYA WAS BURIED, MORE THAN ONE THOUSAND MOURNERS FILED PAST HER COFFIN TO PAY THEIR LAST RESPECTS. DOZENS OF POLITKOVSKAYA'S COLLEAGUES, PUBLIC FIGURES AND ADMIRERS OF HER WORK GATHERED AT THE CEMETERY.

ALTHOUGH THE SUSPECTS WERE FOUND RELATIVELY QUICKLY, IT TOOK EIGHT YEARS AND THREE TRIALS BEFORE ANYONE WAS FOUND GUILTY. IN 2014, A COURT FINALLY SENTENCED TWO MEN TO LIFE IN PRISON FOR POLITKOVSKAYA'S MURDER, AND HANDED LENGTHY PRISON TERMS TO THREE OTHERS INVOLVED IN THE KILLING. IT IS STILL UNCLEAR WHO ORDERED OR PAID FOR THE CONTRACT KILLING.

IT WAS NOT UNTIL THREE DAYS AFTER ANNA POLITKOVSKAYA'S MURDER THAT PUTIN SAID ANYTHING PUBLICLY ABOUT HER DEATH. HE MADE A STATEMENT TO THE MEDIA WHILE IN DRESDEN AFTER A MEETING WITH GERMAN CHANCELLOR ANGELA MERKEL. HE PLAYED DOWN POLITKOVSKAYA'S INFLUENCE AND SUGGESTED THAT HER MURDER WAS DAMAGING TO BOTH THE RUSSIAN GOVERNMENT AND HIMSELF, IMPLYING THAT HE HAD NO MOTIVE TO KILL HER.

THAT JOURNALIST WAS INDEED A HARSH CRITIC OF THE CURRENT RUSSIAN GOVERNMENT, BUT I THINK THAT JOURNALISTS KNOW...

...CERTAINLY, EXPERTS ARE AWARE OF THIS, THAT HER POLITICAL INFLUENCE IN THE COUNTRY WAS EXTREMELY INSIGNIFICANT.

SHE WAS KNOWN IN JOURNALIST CIRCLES AND AMONG HUMAN-RIGHTS ACTIVISTS AND IN THE WEST, BUT HER INFLUENCE ON POLITICS IN RUSSIA WAS MINIMAL. THE MURDER OF SUCH A PERSON — THE COLD-BLOODED MURDER OF A WOMAN, A MOTHER — IS IN ITSELF AN ATTACK ON OUR COUNTRY. THIS MURDER DOES MUCH MORE HARM TO RUSSIA AND ITS CURRENT GOVERNMENT, AND TO THE CURRENT GOVERNMENT IN CHECHNYA, THAN ANY OF HER ARTICLES.

JOURNALISM IN RUSSIA IS A DANGEROUS OCCUPATION. DOZENS OF RUSSIAN JOURNALISTS HAVE BEEN MURDERED OR DIED IN SUSPICIOUS CIRCUMSTANCES SINCE 2000, ACCORDING TO THE COMMITTEE TO PROTECT JOURNALISTS AND THE GLASNOST DEFENSE FOUNDATION.

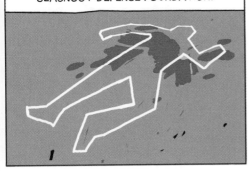

IN NOVEMBER 2009, INDEPENDENT BROADCASTER OLGA KOTOVSKAYA FELL TO HER DEATH FROM A 14TH-FLOOR WINDOW, A DAY AFTER WINNING A LONG-RUNNING COURT BATTLE TO REGAIN CONTROL OF HER SUCCESSFUL KASKAD REGIONAL TV CHANNEL.

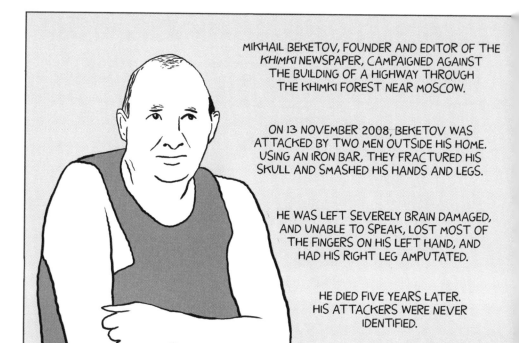

MIKHAIL BEKETOV, FOUNDER AND EDITOR OF THE *KHIMKI* NEWSPAPER, CAMPAIGNED AGAINST THE BUILDING OF A HIGHWAY THROUGH THE KHIMKI FOREST NEAR MOSCOW.

ON 13 NOVEMBER 2008, BEKETOV WAS ATTACKED BY TWO MEN OUTSIDE HIS HOME. USING AN IRON BAR, THEY FRACTURED HIS SKULL AND SMASHED HIS HANDS AND LEGS.

HE WAS LEFT SEVERELY BRAIN DAMAGED, AND UNABLE TO SPEAK, LOST MOST OF THE FINGERS ON HIS LEFT HAND, AND HAD HIS RIGHT LEG AMPUTATED.

HE DIED FIVE YEARS LATER. HIS ATTACKERS WERE NEVER IDENTIFIED.

ON 19 JANUARY 2009, AN ASSAILANT SHOT ANASTASIA BABUROVA, A FREELANCE CORRESPONDENT FOR THE INDEPENDENT NEWSPAPER *NOVAYA GAZETA*, WITHIN WALKING DISTANCE OF THE KREMLIN. BABUROVA'S DEATH WAS LIKELY PROMPTED BY HER RECENT COVERAGE OF PROMINENT HUMAN RIGHTS LAWYER STANISLAV MARKELOV — WHO HAD DENOUNCED THE EARLY RELEASE OF A RUSSIAN ARMY OFFICER CONVICTED IN 2000 FOR THE ABDUCTION AND MURDER OF A CHECHEN GIRL.

THE LAWYER AND JOURNALIST HAD JUST LEFT THE INDEPENDENT PRESS CENTER, WHERE THE NEWS CONFERENCE WAS HELD. THE ASSAILANT SHOT MARKELOV IN THE BACK OF THE HEAD WITH A PISTOL FITTED WITH A SILENCER. BABUROVA TRIED TO STOP THE KILLER AND AS A RESULT WAS ALSO SHOT. THREE NEO-NAZIS WERE CONVICTED OF THE MURDERS.

NOT ALL OF THESE KILLINGS HAD A CONNECTION WITH THE RUSSIAN GOVERNMENT, BUT IT IS CLEAR THAT THE KREMLIN CONSIDERED CRITICAL JOURNALISM UNACCEPTABLE, AND THIS HAS ENCOURAGED OTHERS TO TAKE VIOLENT ACTION AGAINST THOSE IN THE MEDIA.

IT WOULD BE A BRAVE JOURNALIST WHO EXPOSED CRIMES COMMITTED BY THOSE IN AUTHORITY, WHEN DOING SO MEANT BEING FIRED, HARASSED, CALLED A TRAITOR OR MURDERED.

THIS MEANT THAT PUTIN AND HIS KREMLIN ASSOCIATES HAD LITTLE TO FEAR FROM THE RUSSIAN MEDIA AS THEY CONTINUED TO PLUNDER THE COUNTRY.

A MAJOR TARGET OF THE KREMLIN WAS MIKHAIL KHODORKOVSKY, RUSSIA'S RICHEST MAN. ANOTHER YELTSIN-ERA OLIGARCH WHO HAD MADE HIS FORTUNE — ESTIMATED BY FORBES MAGAZINE TO BE MORE THAN $15 BILLION — FROM THE CONTROVERSIAL PRIVATISATION OF SOVIET STATE ASSETS.

KHODORKOVSKY BEGAN HIS CAREER AS A LOYAL SOVIET-ERA COMMUNIST PARTY MEMBER...

...RUNNING A COMPUTER IMPORT BUSINESS UNDER THE WING OF THE PARTY'S YOUTH MOVEMENT (KOMSOMOL).

IN 1987 — FOUR YEARS BEFORE THE FALL OF THE SOVIET UNION — HE FOUNDED MENATAP, WHICH BECAME ONE OF RUSSIA'S FIRST PRIVATE BANKS.

IN THE 1990s, THE BANK ACQUIRED MASSIVE AMOUNTS OF SHARES IN COMPANIES THAT WERE SOLD OFF FROM THE STATE AT BARGAIN PRICES...

...ALL PICKED UP ILLEGALLY, PROSECUTORS WERE TO LATER CLAIM, VIA THE USE OF UMBRELLA COMPANIES.

IN 1995, KHODORKOVSKY BOUGHT YUKOS, THE STATE-OWNED OIL AND GAS COMPANY, FOR A KNOCK-DOWN PRICE OF $350 MILLION.

FROM A POINT OF COLLAPSE, YUKOS THEN BECAME RUSSIA'S SECOND BIGGEST OIL COMPANY, PUMPING OUT ONE IN EVERY FIVE BARRELS THE COUNTRY PRODUCED.

IN THE '90s, KHODORKOVSKY HAD THRIVED UNDER YELTSIN, EVEN SERVING AS DEPUTY FUEL AND OIL MINISTER.

KHODORKOVSKY

BUT ONCE PUTIN CAME TO POWER CONFLICT WITH HIS BRUTAL AUTHORITARIAN REGIME WAS INEVITABLE.

NOT ONLY DID KHODORKOVSKY OWN THE VAST OIL AND GAS RESERVES THAT THE KREMLIN WANTED BACK IN ITS CONTROL...

...BUT HE INTERFERED IN POLITICS. THE OLIGARCH PROVIDED FUNDING TO NEARLY ALL THE POLITICAL PARTIES THAT OPPOSED PUTIN.

IN OCTOBER 2003, KHODORKOVSKY WAS ARRESTED AND CHARGED WITH FRAUD. SHORTLY AFTER THIS THE GOVERNMENT FROZE YUKOS'S SHARES ON TAX CHARGES.

OVER THE DAYS THAT FOLLOWED, THE REST OF RUSSIA'S BILLIONAIRES WATCHED IN HORROR AS PROSECUTORS SEIZED KHODORKOVSKY'S $15 BILLION STAKE IN YUKOS.

KHODORKOVSKY'S TRIAL CONTINUED UNTIL 2005, WHEN HE WAS FOUND GUILTY OF SIX OF THE SEVEN CHARGES FILED AGAINST HIM. HE WAS SENTENCED TO NINE YEARS IN PRISON (LATER REDUCED TO EIGHT YEARS).

JUST BEFORE HE WOULD HAVE BEEN ELIGIBLE FOR PAROLE IN 2007, ADDITIONAL CHARGES OF EMBEZZLEMENT AND MONEY LAUNDERING WERE BROUGHT AGAINST HIM AND HIS SENTENCE WAS EXTENDED FOR A FURTHER SEVEN YEARS.

WHY DIDN'T KHODORKOVSKY FLEE RUSSIA AS VLADIMIR GUSINSKY AND BORIS BEREZOVSKY HAD DONE BEFORE? NOT LONG AFTER HIS RELEASE FROM PRISON, KHODORKOVSKY OFFERED AN EXPLANATION...

SAYING THAT HE HAD ALWAYS BEEN SOMEONE WHO LACKED ANY FEELINGS OF FEAR. HIS FAVOURITE SPORT, FOR EXAMPLE, WAS ROCK-CLIMBING WITHOUT ANY SAFETY EQUIPMENT.

IT WASN'T, HE EXPLAINED, BECAUSE HE'D OVERCOME HIS FEAR. IT WAS BECAUSE HE'D NEVER HAD ANY. THROUGHOUT HIS YEARS IN PRISON HE SLEPT SOUNDLY.

EVEN AFTER HE'D BEEN ATTACKED WITH A KNIFE, HE'D GONE BACK TO HIS BUNK AND HAD NO PROBLEM SLEEPING.

HE FOUND IT STRANGE HIMSELF. PEOPLE ASKED WHETHER HE WORRIED THAT SOMEONE MAY KNIFE HIM IN THE BACK.

BUT HE JUST WASN'T AFRAID.

KHODORKOVSKY WAS RELEASED IN DECEMBER 2013. HE LEFT RUSSIA AND NOW LIVES IN EXILE IN LONDON.

OTHER CRITICS OF PUTIN DID NOT GET OFF SO LIGHTLY.

ALEXANDER LITVINENKO

ALEXANDER LITVINENKO WAS BORN IN THE CITY OF VORONEZH IN 1962.

IN 1980 HE JOINED A MILITARY UNIT WITH THE INTERIOR MINISTRY. EIGHT YEARS LATER, HE MOVED TO THE KGB...

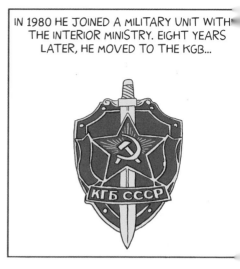

...AND ROSE THROUGH THE RANKS TO LIEUTENANT COLONEL IN THE 1990s, WHEN THE KGB BECAME THE FSB.

HERE, PUTIN BECAME HIS BOSS. BUT THEY REPORTEDLY DIDN'T SEE EYE TO EYE ON CORRUPTION WITHIN THE FSB.

IN 1998, LITVINENKO EXPOSED AN ALLEGED PLOT TO ASSASSINATE THE RUSSIAN OLIGARCH BORIS BEREZOVSKY...

...AND WAS, SOON AFTER, ARRESTED ON CHARGES OF ABUSING HIS OFFICE. HE SPENT NINE MONTHS IN A REMAND CENTRE BEFORE BEING ACQUITTED.

AFTER LEAVING THE FSB, LITVINENKO AND RUSSIAN–AMERICAN HISTORIAN YURI FELSHTINSKY WROTE A BOOK...

...IN WHICH THEY CLAIMED FSB AGENTS WERE RESPONSIBLE FOR THE APARTMENT BLOCK BOMBINGS OF 1999.

LITVINENKO FLED WITH HIS FAMILY TO THE UK IN 2000 (THE YEAR PUTIN BECAME PRESIDENT), CLAIMING PERSECUTION, AND WAS GRANTED ASYLUM. IN LONDON HE WAS EMPLOYED BY MI6 AS AN EXPERT ON RUSSIAN ORGANISED CRIME.

ON 1 NOVEMBER 2006, LITVINENKO MET TWO RUSSIAN MEN AT THE PINE BAR IN LONDON'S MILLENNIUM HOTEL – DMITRY KOVTUN AND ANDREI LUGOVOI, A FORMER KGB OFFICER.

LATER HE ALSO MET ITALIAN ACADEMIC MARIO SCARAMELLA AT AN ITSU SUSHI BAR IN PICCADILLY, LONDON...

...WHERE HE IS SAID TO HAVE RECEIVED INFORMATION ABOUT THE DEATH OF ANNA POLITKOVSKAYA, WHOSE MURDER HAD TAKEN PLACE THREE WEEKS PREVIOUSLY.

WHAT ALEXANDER LITVINENKO DID NOT KNOW IS THAT LUGOVOI AND KOVTUN HAD POISONED HIM. THEY HAD PLACED POLONIUM-210, A HIGHLY RADIOACTIVE ISOTOPE, IN THE TEAPOT DURING THEIR MEETING.

WIDELY HELD OPINION IS THAT THE VISITING KILLERS HAD BEEN SENT BY THE FSB IN AN OPERATION LIKELY TO HAVE BEEN APPROVED BY VLADIMIR PUTIN HIMSELF.

DMITRY KOVTUN   ANDREY LUGOVOI

POLONIUM IS ONE OF THE MOST TOXIC POISONS KNOWN TO MAN WHEN SWALLOWED OR INHALED — MORE THAN 250 BILLION TIMES MORE DEADLY THAN HYDROGEN CYANIDE. THIS LETHAL SUBSTANCE HAD COME FROM A RUSSIAN NUCLEAR REACTOR.

LUGOVOI AND KOVTUN HAD NO IDEA WHAT THEY WERE CARRYING. THEIR BEHAVIOUR IN BRITAIN BORDERED ON THE SUICIDAL AND SUGGESTED THAT NOBODY IN MOSCOW HAD TOLD THEM THAT POLONIUM WAS RADIOACTIVE.

POLONIUM LEFT A TRACE, PLACING THE TWO MEN IN SPECIFIC LOCATIONS AND INDICATING, VIA ALPHA-RADIATION MARKINGS, WHO SAT WHERE.

IT WAS POSSIBLE TO IDENTIFY ANYTHING AND EVERYTHING THE ASSASSINS TOUCHED.

LITVINENKO'S CERAMIC TEAPOT GAVE OFF READINGS OF 100,000 BECQUERELS PER CENTIMETRE SQUARED. THE BIGGEST READING CAME FROM THE SPOUT.

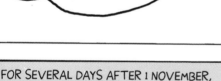

THE TEAPOT HAD BEEN RUN THROUGH THE DISHWASHER AFTERWARDS AND WAS UNKNOWINGLY REUSED FOR OTHER CUSTOMERS.

FOR SEVERAL DAYS AFTER 1 NOVEMBER, LITVINENKO EXPERIENCED SEVERE VOMITING.

AT ONE POINT, HE COULD NOT WALK WITHOUT ASSISTANCE. AFTER THREE DAYS OF SICKNESS AND STOMACH PAINS LITVINENKO WAS ADMITTED TO BARNET GENERAL HOSPITAL, NORTH LONDON.

17 NOVEMBER

LITVINENKO IS TRANSFERRED TO UNIVERSITY COLLEGE HOSPITAL, IN CENTRAL LONDON. HE BEGINS TO LOSE HIS HAIR.

AS HIS CONDITION WORSENS, HE IS PLACED UNDER ARMED POLICE GUARD.

20 NOVEMBER

LITVINENKO IS MOVED TO INTENSIVE CARE. SCOTLAND YARD'S COUNTER-TERRORISM UNIT TAKES OVER THE INVESTIGATION.

THE KREMLIN DISMISSES ALLEGATIONS THAT THE RUSSIAN GOVERNMENT POISONED LITVINENKO.

22 NOVEMBER

HE HAS A HEART ATTACK.

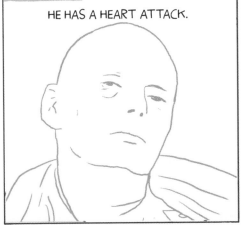

23 NOVEMBER

HE DIES IN INTENSIVE CARE.

A DAY OR TWO BEFORE HE SLIPPED INTO A COMA, LITVINENKO DICTATED A STATEMENT THAT HE ASKED TO BE RELEASED IN THE EVENT OF HIS DEATH.

AS I LIE HERE, I SENSE THE DISTINCT PRESENCE OF THE ANGEL OF DEATH. IT IS STILL POSSIBLE I'LL BE ABLE TO EVADE HIM, BUT I FEAR MY FEET ARE NO LONGER AS FAST AS THEY USED TO BE.

I THINK THE TIME HAS COME TO SAY A FEW WORDS TO THE MAN RESPONSIBLE FOR MY CURRENT CONDITION. YOU MAY BE ABLE TO FORCE ME TO STAY QUIET, BUT THIS SILENCE WILL COME AT A PRICE TO YOU. YOU HAVE NOW PROVED THAT YOU ARE EXACTLY THE RUTHLESS BARBARIAN YOUR HARSHEST CRITICS MADE YOU OUT TO BE.

YOU HAVE DEMONSTRATED THAT YOU HAVE NO RESPECT FOR HUMAN LIFE, LIBERTY, OR OTHER VALUES OF CIVILISATION. YOU HAVE SHOWN THAT YOU DO NOT DESERVE TO HOLD YOUR POST, AND YOU DO NOT DESERVE THE TRUST OF CIVILISED PEOPLE.

YOU MAY BE ABLE TO SHUT ONE MAN UP, BUT THE NOISE OF PROTEST ALL OVER THE WORLD WILL REVERBERATE IN YOUR EARS, MR PUTIN, TO THE END OF YOUR LIFE. MAY GOD FORGIVE YOU FOR WHAT YOU HAVE DONE, NOT ONLY TO ME BUT TO MY BELOVED RUSSIA AND HER PEOPLE.

FOR REASONS THE BRITISH POLICE DID NOT DISCLOSE, THEY IDENTIFIED LUGOVOI AS THE MURDER SUSPECT AND KOVTUN AS A WITNESS.

RUSSIA REFUSED EXTRADITION REQUEST FOR LUGOVOI; MOREOVER, HE WAS MADE A MEMBER OF PARLIAMENT, GIVING HIM IMMUNITY FROM PROSECUTION, INCLUDING EXTRADITION REQUESTS.

ON 10 DECEMBER 2007, THE BRITISH AMBASSADOR IN MOSCOW, TONY BRENTON, VOICED REGRET OVER THE ELECTION OF LUGOVOI TO THE DUMA, SAYING:

IT IS A PITY THAT A MAN WANTED FOR MURDER GAINS POLITICAL RECOGNITION. IT DOES RUSSIA NO GOOD AT ALL TO HAVE LUGOVOI THERE IN THE PARLIAMENT, IT CONTINUES THE SUSPICION. IF HE STEPS A FOOT OUT OF RUSSIA HE WILL BE ARRESTED. WE WANT HIM.

ON THE RELEASE OF THE EVENTUAL REPORT ON THE MURDER IN 2016, BRITISH LABOUR MP IAN AUSTIN SAID:

PUTIN IS AN UNRECONSTRUCTED KGB THUG AND GANGSTER WHO MURDERS HIS OPPONENTS IN RUSSIA AND HERE, AS WE KNOW, ON THE STREETS OF LONDON – AND NOTHING ANNOUNCED TODAY IS GOING TO MAKE THE BLINDEST BIT OF DIFFERENCE.

AS PUTIN NEARED THE END OF HIS SECOND TERM AS PRESIDENT, HE FACED A PROBLEM. HE WAS BARRED FROM A THIRD CONSECUTIVE TERM BY THE CONSTITUTION.

THE SOLUTION INVOLVED A MAN CALLED DMITRY MEDVEDEV.

MEDVEDEV, A QUIETLY SPOKEN LAWYER, HAD WORKED ON LEGAL ISSUES FOR PUTIN SINCE THE ST PETERSBURG DAYS, INCLUDING ON THE FALLOUT OF THE OIL-FOR-FOOD SCANDAL. HE HAD A REPUTATION FOR ZEALOUS PRECISION, BUT ALSO FOR TIMIDITY. AFTER PUTIN BECAME ACTING PRESIDENT OF RUSSIA IN DECEMBER 1999, HE MADE MEDVEDEV HIS PROTÉGÉ.

IN 2000, MEDVEDEV HEADED PUTIN'S FIRST PRESIDENTIAL ELECTION CAMPAIGN AND, FOLLOWING HIS VICTORY, BECAME PUTIN'S FIRST DEPUTY CHIEF OF STAFF.

IN 2003, MEDVEDEV WAS PROMOTED TO CHIEF OF STAFF, AND TWO YEARS LATER WAS APPOINTED TO THE NEWLY CREATED POST OF FIRST DEPUTY PRIME MINISTER.

IN DECEMBER 2007, PUTIN NAMED DMITRY MEDVEDEV AS HIS SUCCESSOR TO TAKE OVER AS PRESIDENT.

IN MARCH 2008, MEDVEDEV WON THE PRESIDENTIAL ELECTION WITH SEVENTY PER CENT OF THE VOTE.

ONCE IN OFFICE HE IMMEDIATELY APPOINTED VLADIMIR PUTIN AS HIS PRIME MINISTER.

MOST RUSSIANS BELIEVED THAT PUTIN AND HIS CIRCLE WERE STILL RUNNING THE COUNTRY.

THE FIRST CRISIS MEDVEDEV FACED CONCERNED GEORGIA. IN AUGUST 2008, TENSIONS BETWEEN GEORGIA AND RUSSIA OVER BREAKAWAY TERRITORIES ABKHAZIA AND SOUTH OSSETIA BOILED OVER INTO WAR.

THE CONFLICT CAME AFTER MONTHS OF BUILD-UP IGNITED BY GEORGIA'S PUSH TO MOVE TOWARDS EVENTUAL NATO MEMBERSHIP.

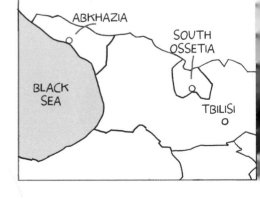

WHEN GEORGIAN PRESIDENT MIKHEIL SAAKASHVILI ORDERED HIS TROOPS TO CAPTURE THE SOUTH OSSETIAN CAPITAL OF TSKHINVALI, RUSSIA CAME TO ITS DEFENCE. TROOPS WERE MOVED TO THE BORDER AND AIR STRIKES CONDUCTED ON GEORGIAN POSITIONS IN SOUTH OSSETIA AND ABKHAZIA.

ALTHOUGH THE UNITED STATES, GREAT BRITAIN AND NATO CALLED FOR A CEASEFIRE, THE CONFLICT CONTINUED FOR FIVE DAYS. RUSSIA QUICKLY TOOK CONTROL OF TSKHINVALI AND ROLLED ITS TANKS AND TROOPS THROUGH OSSETIA INTO GEORGIA, STOPPING ONLY 30 MILES FROM THE GEORGIAN CAPITAL, TBILISI.

THE FIGHTING ENDED IN TRIUMPH FOR RUSSIA AND HUMILIATION FOR GEORGIA. SEVERAL HUNDRED PEOPLE WERE KILLED IN THE CONFLICT AND THOUSANDS OF ETHNIC GEORGIANS DISPLACED.

ALTHOUGH RUSSIA EVENTUALLY WITHDREW FROM GEORGIA, IT RETAINED A MILITARY PRESENCE IN BOTH SOUTH OSSETIA AND THE SEPARATIST REGION OF ABKHAZIA.

AT THE UNITED RUSSIA CONGRESS IN MOSCOW IN SEPTEMBER 2011, MEDVEDEV OFFICIALLY PROPOSED THAT PUTIN STAND FOR THE PRESIDENCY IN 2012.

PUTIN WON RE-ELECTION WITH OVER 60 PER CENT OF THE VOTE AFTER A DECISION TO EXTEND PRESIDENTIAL TERMS FROM FOUR TO SIX YEARS.

MEDVEDEV RETURNED TO HIS POST AS PRIME MINISTER. THE ELECTION SPARKED LARGE ANTI-PUTIN PROTESTS WITH CRITICS ALLEGING VOTER FRAUD. TENS OF THOUSANDS FILLED THE STREETS IN MOSCOW AND OTHER RUSSIAN CITIES.

ПУТИН
ДОЛЖЕН
УЙТИ
PUTIN MUST
GO

ON FEBRUARY 2012, RUSSIAN FEMINIST PUNK ROCK GROUP PUSSY RIOT STAGED A PERFORMANCE INSIDE MOSCOW'S CATHEDRAL OF CHRIST THE SAVIOUR.

RIOT FOR RIGHTS

THE GROUP SPECIALISED IN UNAUTHORISED PROVOCATIVE GUERRILLA PERFORMANCES IN PUBLIC PLACES...

...THAT WERE FILMED AS MUSIC VIDEOS AND POSTED ON THE INTERNET.

PUSSY RIOT'S THEMES INCLUDED FEMINISM, LGBTQI+ RIGHTS, AND OPPOSITION TO PRESIDENT VLADIMIR PUTIN AND HIS POLICIES.

A MONTH AFTER THE CATHEDRAL STUNT, ALL WERE ARRESTED AND CHARGED WITH 'HOOLIGANISM MOTIVATED BY RELIGIOUS HATRED'.

FROM MARCH TO JULY THEY WERE HELD WITHOUT BAIL AND WERE THEN CONVICTED AND SENTENCED TO TWO YEARS IN PRISON. SAMUTSEVICH WAS FREED ON PROBATION IN OCTOBER 2012, BUT BOTH TOLOKONNIKOVA AND ALYOKHINA REMAINED IN JAIL. THEIR SENTENCES WERE DUE TO END IN MARCH 2014...

...BUT THEY WERE RELEASED IN DECEMBER 2013 AS PART OF AN AMNESTY, ALONG WITH AT LEAST 2000 OTHER PRISONERS.

THIS AMNESTY WAS A CLEAR BID TO AVOID CONTROVERSY BEFORE RUSSIA'S HOSTING OF THE 2014 WINTER OLYMPICS.

MARIA ALYOKHINA OF PUSSY RIOT TOLD A RUSSIAN TV CHANNEL THAT THE AMNESTY WAS A PR STUNT AND SHE WOULD RATHER HAVE REMAINED IN PRISON.

PUTIN'S REGIME ROUTINELY OPPRESSES IMMIGRANTS AND MINORITIES USING THE EXCUSE THAT IT IS DEFENDING CHRISTIAN VALUES AGAINST THE LIBERAL SECULARISM OF THE WEST.

LGBTQI+ PEOPLE FACE PARTICULAR ADVERSITY IN RUSSIA, WHERE THERE IS WIDESPREAD VIOLENCE FROM PRIVATE INDIVIDUALS, STATE AGENTS, AND VIGILANTE GROUPS.

IN 2013, THE NOTORIOUS FEDERAL LAW PROHIBITING THE 'PROPAGANDA OF NON-TRADITIONAL SEXUAL RELATIONS' AMONG MINORS WAS PASSED.

SOME RUSSIANS ARE GAY. GET OVER IT!

THIS LAW BANNED ANY COMMUNICATION ABOUT THE EXISTENCE OF LGBTQI+ PEOPLE,
OR LGBTQI+ ISSUES TO CHILDREN, BOTH IN THE MEDIA, OR ONLINE.

SAME-SEX COUPLES IN RUSSIA ARE PROHIBITED BY LAW FROM ADOPTING CHILDREN,
AND PEOPLE FROM COUNTRIES THAT ALLOW SAME-SEX MARRIAGE ARE BANNED
FROM ADOPTING RUSSIAN ORPHANS.

THESE LAWS SENT A STRONG AND DISHONEST MESSAGE —
THAT LGBTQI+ PEOPLE ARE A THREAT TO CHILDREN.

BETWEEN FEBRUARY AND APRIL 2017, THERE WERE
A SERIES OF ANTI-GAY PURGES IN THE CHECHEN
REPUBLIC, STILL PART OF THE RUSSIAN
FEDERATION. CHECHNYA'S LAW ENFORCEMENT
AND SECURITY OFFICIALS ROUNDED UP DOZENS
OF MEN ON SUSPICION OF BEING GAY. FOR DAYS,
THEY HELD THEM IN UNOFFICIAL DETENTION
CENTRES, WHILE STARVING, TORTURING
AND ROUTINELY HUMILIATING THEM.

SOME MEN WERE RETURNED TO THEIR FAMILIES BARELY ALIVE FROM BEATINGS.

THEIR CAPTORS OUTED THEM TO THEIR FAMILIES AS GAY AND ENCOURAGED RELATIVES TO CARRY OUT HONOUR KILLINGS.

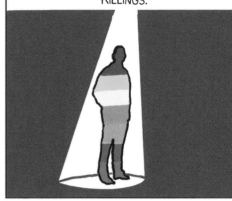

CHECHEN LEADER RAMZAN KADYROV DENIED THE ROUND-UPS, DESPITE EVIDENCE THAT TOP-LEVEL LOCAL AUTHORITIES SANCTIONED THEM.

ANOTHER ROUND OF PURGES TOOK PLACE A YEAR LATER.

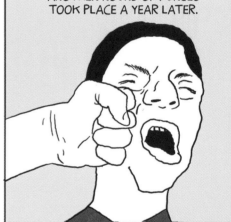

THE RUSSIAN GOVERNMENT'S ANTI-GAY POLICIES ARE THE FLIP SIDE OF PUTIN'S ABSURD MACHO POSTERING AND NEED TO PORTRAY HIMSELF AS A PATRIOTIC STRONGMAN...

...DEDICATED TO REVERSING THE PERCEIVE EMASCULATION OF THE YELTSIN YEARS AND RESTORING RUSSIA'S MASCULINE PRIDE

THE WAVE OF PROTESTS THAT BEGAN IN 2011, WHICH THE MEDIA CALLED THE SNOW REVOLUTION, CONTINUED UNTIL 2013.

A LEADING FIGURE IN THESES PROTESTS WAS THE BRILLIANT AND ENERGETIC BORIS NEMTSOV.

NEMTSOV WAS A PHYSICIST BEFORE BECOMING A POLITICIAN, WORKING AT THE GORKY RADIOPHYSICAL RESEARCH INSTITUTE.

HE WAS ELECTED TO THE SOVIET CONGRESS OF PEOPLE'S DEPUTIES IN 1990. BORIS YELTSIN THEN SELECTED HIM TO BE GOVERNOR OF THE NIZHNY NOVGOROD REGION FROM 1991—97...

...AFTER WHICH HE BECAME FIRST DEPUTY PRIME MINISTER, AND WAS IN CHARGE OF THE ENERGY SECTOR UNTIL 1998.

HE RESIGNED FROM THE LATTER POST AMID A NATIONAL FINANCIAL CRISIS. HE LATER SERVED (2005—06) AS AN ECONOMIC ADVISER TO UKRAINIAN PRESIDENT VIKTOR YUSHCHENKO.

NEMTSOV WAS BRIEFLY A CANDIDATE FOR THE PRESIDENCY OF RUSSIA IN THE 2008 ELECTION, BUT WITHDREW, BECAUSE HE DID NOT WANT TO DRAW LIBERAL VOTES AWAY FROM THE OTHER CANDIDATES.

IN DECEMEBER 2008, NEMTSOV AND RUSSIAN CHESS GRANDMASTER GARRY KASPAROV CO-FOUNDED THE POLITICAL OPPOSITION MOVEMENT SOLIDARNOST (SOLIDARITY). THE ORGANISATION HOPED TO UNITE THE OPPOSITION FORCES IN RUSSIA.

AT A SOLIDARNOST MEETING IN 2009, NEMTSOV ANNOUNCED THAT HE WOULD RUN FOR MAYOR OF SOCHI.

NEMTSOV CRITICISED THE DECISION TO HOLD A WINTER OLYMPICS IN SOCHI. HE POINTED OUT HOW ABSURD IT WAS TO HOLD AN OLYMPICS IN ONE OF ONLY PLACES IN RUSSIA WHERE THERE IS NO SNOW IN THE WINTER.

SOCHI IS SUBTROPICAL, HE SAID, AND HAS NO TRADITION OF SKATING OR HOCKEY. IT IS A CITY WHERE THE PEOPLE PREFER FOOTBALL AND VOLLEYBALL.

THE CONSTRUCTION AT THE OLYMPICS SITE WAS 'DISASTROUS' FOR THE LOCAL ECONOMY, HE ADDED, SAYING THAT ABOUT 5,000 CITIZENS HAD BEEN REMOVED FROM THEIR HOMES TO BUILD OLYMPIC FACILITIES.

HE WENT ON TO DESCRIBE HOW, DUE TO THE CORRUPTION AND INCOMPETENCE OF THE AUTHORITIES, MANY OF THESE PEOPLE HAD NOT BEEN ADEQUATELY COMPENSATED FOR THEIR PROPERTY OR BEEN GIVEN HOUSING ELSEWHERE. BILLIONS OF DOLLARS HAD JUST VANISHED.

MEANWHILE, IN THE UKRAINE... VIKTOR YANUKOVYCH – WHO HAD LOST THE 2004 UKRAINIAN PRESIDENTIAL CAMPAIGN TO VIKTOR YUSHCHENKO (THE MAN FACIALLY-SCARRED AFTER BEING POISONED) – FINALLY WON THE PRESIDENCY, IN 2010.

BUT BY 2013 BOTH HE AND HIS COUNTRY WERE IN DIFFICULTY.

YANUKOVYCH WANTED TO KEEP CLOSE TIES WITH RUSSIA.

HE WAS PUTIN'S MAN IN THE UKRAINE, AND HE ACTED ACCORDINGLY. WHEN HE REFUSED TO SIGN AN ASSOCIATION AGREEMENT WITH THE EUROPEAN UNION IN NOVEMBER 2013, THE COUNTRY BECAME GRIPPED BY UNREST.

JOIN US.

NO.

AN ORGANISED POLITICAL MOVEMENT KNOWN AS 'EUROMAIDAN' DEMANDED CLOSER TIES WITH THE EUROPEAN UNION, AND THE OUSTING OF YANUKOVYCH.

HOWEVER, SOME PEOPLE IN LARGELY RUSSOPHONE EASTERN AND SOUTHERN UKRAINE, THE TRADITIONAL BASES OF SUPPORT FOR YANUKOVYCH, BEGAN TO PROTEST IN FAVOUR OF CLOSER TIES WITH RUSSIA.

WEST CENTER EAST SOUTH

VARIOUS DEMONSTRATIONS WERE HELD IN CRIMEA IN FAVOUR OF LEAVING UKRAINE AND JOINING THE RUSSIAN FEDERATION.

DONETSK

ODESSA

CRIMEA

SEVASTOPOL

BLACK SEA

MORE THAN 70 PEOPLE WERE KILLED IN CLASHES WITH POLICE AND SECURITY FORCES IN FEBRUARY 2014, AS THE REMAINING SUPPORT FOR YANUKOVYCH AND HIS ADMINISTRATION CRUMBLED.

ON 22 FEBRUARY, THE PARLIAMENT VOTED TO IMPEACH YANUKOVYCH. WHEN HE DENOUNCED THE ACTION AS A COUP AND FLED THE CAPITAL, PROTESTORS STORMED HIS RESIDENCE OUTSIDE KIEV AND THE UKRAINIAN GOVERNMENT ISSUED A WARRANT FOR HIS ARREST — ON THE CHARGE OF MASS MURDER.

PUT THESE ON.

NO.

DAYS AFTER YANUKOVICH ARRIVED IN RUSSIA, ARMED MEN OPPOSED TO THE EUROMAIDAN MOVEMENT BEGAN TO TAKE CONTROL OF THE CRIMEAN PENINSULA.

CHECKPOINTS WERE ESTABLISHED BY RUSSIAN SOLDIERS IN UNMARKED GREEN UNIFORMS — KNOWN BY THE LOCAL POPULATION AND THE MEDIA AS 'LITTLE GREEN MEN'.

AFTER THE OCCUPATION OF THE CRIMEAN PARLIAMENT BY THESE TROOPS, (ACTUALLY RUSSIAN SPECIAL FORCES), THE CRIMEAN LEADERSHIP ANNOUNCED A REFERENDUM ON SECESSION FROM UKRAINE.

THIS HEAVILY DISPUTED REFERENDUM WAS FOLLOWED BY THE ANNEXATION OF CRIMEA BY THE RUSSIAN FEDERATION IN MID–MARCH 2014.

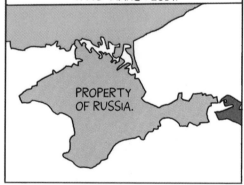

PROPERTY OF RUSSIA.

A MILITARY CONFLICT THEN BEGAN IN EASTERN UKRAINE BETWEEN UKRAINIAN SOLDIERS AND RUSSIAN–BACKED SEPARATISTS. THIS CONTINUED UNTIL 2018. MORE THAN 10,000 PEOPLE WERE KILLED.

BORIS NEMTSOV WAS AMONG THE FEW RUSSIAN STATESMEN TO CRITICISE THE ANNEXATION AND WAR. HE VIEWED CRIMEA AS AN INTEGRAL PART OF UKRAINE, AND HE CONSIDERED ITS ANNEXATION TO BE ILLEGAL.

LATE IN THE EVENING ON 27 FEBRUARY 2015, AS NEMTSOV AND ANNA DURITSKAYA, HIS UKRAINIAN GIRLFRIEND, CROSSED THE BOLSHOY MOSKVORETSKY BRIDGE NEAR THE KREMLIN, A GUNMAN SHOT NEMTSOV SEVERAL TIMES IN THE HEAD AND BACK.

FIVE CHECHEN MEN WERE FOUND GUILTY OF CARRYING OUT THE CONTRACT KILLING FOR 15 MILLION ROUBLES, (AROUND $200,000).

ONE SUSPECT, ANZOR GUBASHEV, WHO WAS THE GETAWAY DRIVER, TOLD INVESTIGATORS THAT NEMTSOV WAS...

CARRYING OUT A POLICY AGAINST OUR STATE, SUPPORTING THE WEST AND DEFAMING OUR GOVERNMENT.

GUBASHEV ALSO MENTIONED RUSSIA'S STANDOFF WITH THE WEST OVER UKRAINE, AND CALLED NEMTSOV AN AGENT OF THE CIA AND OBAMA.

WE DON'T FEEL THE LEAST BIT SORRY THAT WE TOOK HIM OUT, BECAUSE FROM THE VERY BEGINNING HE WAS A WESTERN PROSTITUTE, AND WAS CAUSING ALL SORTS OF CHAOS.

WHETHER THE CHECHEN LEADERSHIP WERE RESPONSIBLE FOR NEMTSOV'S DEATH OR WHETHER THEY ACTED ON BEHALF OF PUTIN IS NOT CLEAR, BUT THE ASSASSINATION OF SUCH A PROMINENT OPPOSITION POLITICAL FIGURE WAS CONVENIENT FOR BOTH PARTIES.

ZHANNA NEMTSOVA, NEMTSOV'S DAUGHTER, HAD THIS TO SAY ABOUT HER FATHER'S DEATH...

HE WAS, FOR ONE DECADE, THE MOST PROMINENT CRITIC OF PUTIN. HE WAS THE MOST POWERFUL LEADER OF THE OPPOSITION IN RUSSIA. AFTER HIS DEATH, THE OPPOSITION IS BEHEADED AND EVERYBODY IS FRIGHTENED — PEOPLE AND POLITICIANS, BOTH OF THEM. AND NOW WE DO NOT HAVE ANY OTHER OPPOSITION FIGURE IN RUSSIA SO POWERFUL AND SO BRAVE AND SO CLEVER.

SHE IS IN NO DOUBT THAT THE MURDER WAS ORDERED BY PUTIN HIMSELF.

IN RUSSIA, THE INVASION AND ANNEXATION OF CRIMEA WAS WILDLY POPULAR. PUTIN'S APPROVAL RATINGS SHOT UP ABOVE 70 PERCENT.

AT THE END OF MARCH 2014 PRESIDENT BARACK OBAMA MET WITH OTHER NATO LEADERS IN BRUSSELS TO DISCUSS RUSSIA AND UKRAINE.

MUCH LIKE HIS PREDECESSOR, GEORGE W BUSH, HE DID NOT SEE THE DANGER.

THIS IS NOT ANOTHER COLD WAR THAT WE'RE ENTERING INTO. AFTER ALL, UNLIKE THE SOVIET UNION, RUSSIA LEADS NO BLOC OF NATIONS, NO GLOBAL IDEOLOGY.

OBAMA, LIKE OTHER WESTERN LEADERS, HAD MISSED PUTIN'S TRANSFORMATION FROM A BUREAUCRAT WHO HAD BEEN ENTRUSTED WITH A HUGE COUNTRY INTO A MEGALOMANIACAL DICTATOR.

ON 17 JULY 2014, MALAYSIA AIRLINES FLIGHT MH17, EN ROUTE FROM AMSTERDAM TO KUALA LUMPUR, WAS TRAVELLING OVER CONFLICT-HIT UKRAINE WHEN IT DISAPPEARED FROM RADAR.

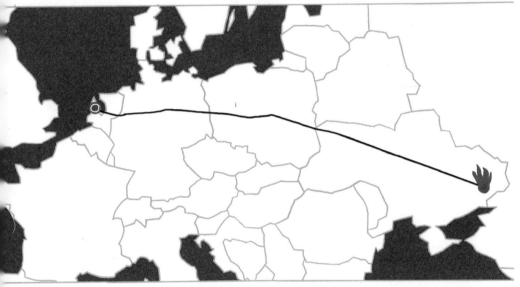

THE PLANE CRASHED AFTER BEING HIT BY A RUSSIAN-MADE BUK MISSILE OVER EASTERN UKRAINE. THERE WERE NO SURVIVORS. IN SEPTEMBER 2016, FOLLOWING AN INTERNATIONAL VESTIGATION, EVIDENCE SHOWED THE BUK MISSILE HAD COME FROM RUSSIAN TERRITORY AND HAD BEEN FIRED FROM A FIELD CONTROLLED BY RUSSIAN-BACKED SEPARATISTS.

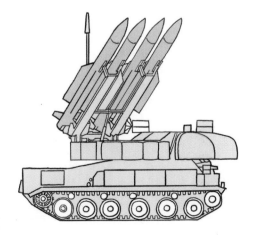

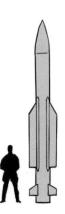

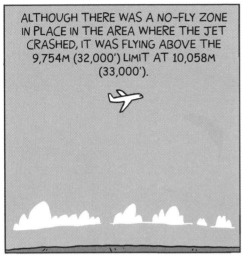

ALTHOUGH THERE WAS A NO-FLY ZONE IN PLACE IN THE AREA WHERE THE JET CRASHED, IT WAS FLYING ABOVE THE 9,754M (32,000') LIMIT AT 10,058M (33,000').

THAT DAY WAS BUSY FOR THE EASTERN UKRAINE AIRSPACE — WITH ONE HUNDRED AND SIXTY COMMERCIAL FLIGHTS FLYING OVER THE REGION.

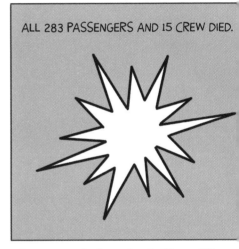

ALL 283 PASSENGERS AND 15 CREW DIED.

THE CREW WERE ALL MALAYSIAN, WHILE OVER TWO-THIRDS OF THE PASSENGERS WERE DUTCH. MOST OF THE OTHER PASSENGERS WERE MALAYSIANS AND AUSTRALIANS. THE REMAINDER WERE CITIZENS OF SEVEN OTHER COUNTRIES. AMONG THE PASSENGERS WERE DELEGATES EN ROUTE TO THE 20TH INTERNATIONAL AIDS CONFERENCE IN MELBOURNE.

...INCLUDING JOEP LANGE, A FORMER PRESIDENT OF THE INTERNATIONAL AIDS SOCIETY.

ALSO ON BOARD WERE DUTCH SENATOR WILLEM WITTEVEEN, HIS WIFE LIDWIEN HEERKENS AND THEIR DAUGHTER MARIT WITTEVEEN...

...AUSTRALIAN AUTHOR LIAM DAVISON AND HIS WIFE FRANKIE DAVISON...

...AND MALAYSIAN ACTRESS SHUBA JAY, HER HUSBAND PAUL GOES AND THEIR DAUGHTER KAELA MAYA JAY GOES.

NONE OF THESE PEOPLE HAD ANYTHING TO DO WITH THE UKRAINE CONFLICT. AT LEAST 20 FAMILY GROUPS WERE ON THE AIRCRAFT. EIGHTY PASSENGERS WERE UNDER THE AGE OF 18.

DUTCH PROSECUTORS ALLEGED THAT FOUR MEN WERE RESPONSIBLE FOR THE MISSILE LAUNCH: THE RUSSIANS IGOR GIRKIN, FORMER COLONEL IN RUSSIA'S FSB...

...SERGEI DUBINSKY, EMPLOYED BY RUSSIA'S GRU MILITARY INTELLIGENCE AGENCY...

...OLEG PULATOV, FORMER SOLDIER WITH GRU'S SPECIAL FORCES SPETSNAZ UNIT...

AND THE UKRAINIAN LEONID KHARCHENKO COMMANDER OF A COMBAT UNIT IN DONETSK.

ALL WERE SENIOR COMMANDERS FIGHTING UKRAINIAN FORCES IN THE RUSSIAN-BACKED DONETSK PEOPLE'S REPUBLIC. THE CASE WAS TRIED IN ABSENTIA AS RUSSIA DOES NOT EXTRADITE ITS CITIZENS.

PUTIN HAS CONSISTENTLY DENIED THAT RUSSIA HAD ANY INVOLVEMENT IN THE SHOOTING DOWN OF FLIGHT MH17, CLAIMING THAT THE UKRAINIAN AIR FORCE WAS RESPONSIBLE.

BUT THERE IS NO EVIDENCE TO SUPPORT THIS VIEW AND PLENTY THAT THE PLANE WAS SHOT DOWN FROM THE GROUND AND FROM A SEPARATIST-HELD AREA.

INVESTIGATORS PINPOINTED THE LAUNCH SITE ON A HILL IN FARMLAND WEST OF PERVOMAISKYI, HAVING TRACED THE CONVOY CARRYING THE BUK FROM THE RUSSIAN BORDER THROUGH DONETSK, TOREZ, SNIZHNE AND ON TO THE LAUNCH SITE IN THE HOURS BEFORE MH17 WAS DOWNED.

ON 20 DECEMBER 2017, THE INTELLIGENCE AND SECURITY COMMITTEE OF THE UK PARLIAMENT PUBLISHED ITS ANNUAL REPORT. IT CONTAINED A SHORT SECTION ENTITLED 'RUSSIAN OBJECTIVES AND ACTIVITY AGAINST UK AND ALLIED INTERESTS' WHICH QUOTES MI6 AS STATING...

'RUSSIA CONDUCTS INFORMATION WARFARE ON A MASSIVE SCALE... AN EARLY EXAMPLE OF THIS WAS A HUGELY INTENSIVE, MULTI-CHANNEL PROPAGANDA EFFORT TO PERSUADE THE WORLD THAT RUSSIA BORE NO RESPONSIBILITY FOR THE SHOOTING DOWN OF MH17...

...AN OUTRIGHT FALSEHOOD: WE KNOW BEYOND ANY REASONABLE DOUBT THAT THE RUSSIAN MILITARY SUPPLIED AND SUBSEQUENTLY RECOVERED THE MISSILE LAUNCHER.'

AS WELL AS THE CONTINUING WAR IN UKRAINE, RUSSIA ALSO
BECAME INVOLVED IN A CONFLICT IN THE MIDDLE EAST.

IN MARCH 2011, SYRIA'S GOVERNMENT, LED BY
PRESIDENT BASHAR AL-ASSAD, FACED A
CHALLENGE TO ITS AUTHORITY WHEN
PRO-DEMOCRACY PROTESTS ERUPTED
THROUGHOUT THE COUNTRY.

THE SYRIAN GOVERNMENT BRUTALLY
SUPPRESSED THE DEMONSTRATIONS,
MAKING EXTENSIVE USE OF POLICE,
MILITARY, AND PARAMILITARY FORCES.

DESPITE THE REGIME'S BRUTALITY, OPPOSITION
CONTINUED. IT WASN'T UNTIL 2015 THAT
PUTIN RESPONDED TO AL-ASSAD'S
CALL FOR ASSISTANCE.

ON 30 SEPTEMBER 2015, FOLLOWING AN FFICIAL REQUEST BY ASSAD FOR MILITARY AID AGAINST REBEL GROUPS, RUSSIA CARRIED OUT AIRSTRIKES ON SYRIA.

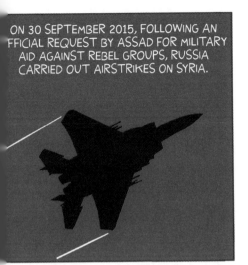

THE GOAL, PUTIN SAID, WAS TO COMBAT THE TERROR ORGANISATION 'ISLAMIC STATE'. BUT, IN PRACTICE, THEY ALSO ATTACKED OTHER ANTI-ASSAD REBELS, SOME OF WHICH WERE BACKED BY THE WEST.

TO JUSTIFY THE RUSSIAN INTERVENTION, PUTIN POINTED A FINGER AT THE UNITED STATES, NO STRANGER TO MIDDLE EASTERN WARS, MOST OF WHICH RUSSIA HAD OPPOSED.

HOW DID IT ACTUALLY TURN OUT? RATHER THAN BRINGING ABOUT REFORMS, AN AGGRESSIVE FOREIGN INTERFERENCE [BY THE US] HAS RESULTED IN A BRAZEN DESTRUCTION OF NATIONAL INSTITUTIONS.

INSTEAD OF THE TRIUMPH OF DEMOCRACY AND PROGRESS, WE GOT VIOLENCE, POVERTY, AND SOCIAL DISASTER. NOBODY CARES A BIT ABOUT HUMAN RIGHTS, INCLUDING THE RIGHT TO LIFE.

TO PREVENT THE SAME ATROCITY FROM HAPPENING IN SYRIA, HIS ARGUMENT WENT, RUSSIA WOULD NEED TO INVOLVE ITSELF.

BUT NOW, MORE THAN FIVE YEARS ON, RUSSIA HAS DONE EXACTLY WHAT PUTIN SAID HE WOULD NOT DO – CREATED VIOLENCE, POVERTY AND SOCIAL DISASTER.

SYRIA HAS SEEN NOTHING BUT 'BRAZEN DESTRUCTION', NOTABLY IN THE BRUTAL ASSAULT ON ALEPPO IN 2016, WHICH REDUCED THE CITY TO RUBBLE.

AS FOR HUMAN RIGHTS, THE ASSAD GOVERNMENT, WHOSE TORTURE OF PROTESTERS INCITED THE CIVIL WAR, REMAINS IN POWER. WAR MONITOR 'SYRIAN OBSERVATORY FOR HUMAN RIGHTS' SAID ON 4 JANUARY 2020 THAT OVER 380,000 PEOPLE HAVE BEEN KILLED SINCE THE WAR STARTED.

MORE THAN HALF OF SYRIA'S POPULATION HAS BEEN DISPLACED OVER THE COURSE OF THE CONFLICT — AMOUNTING TO AROUND 12 MILLION PEOPLE.

ACCORDING TO AMNESTY INTERNATIONAL, IN LATE FEBRUARY 2016 RUSSIAN WARPLANES DELIBERATELY TARGETED CIVILIANS AND RESCUE WORKERS DURING THEIR BOMBING CAMPAIGN.

TIRANA HASSAN, DIRECTOR OF AMNESTY'S CRISIS RESPONSE PROGRAMME, SAID...

WE'VE DOCUMENTED STRIKES ON SCHOOLS, STRIKES ON HOSPITALS AND CIVILIAN HOMES. ONE OF THE MOST EGREGIOUS PARTS OF WHAT RUSSIA AND THE SYRIAN FORCES ARE DOING IS LOOPING AROUND INJURING AND KILLING HUMANITARIAN WORKERS AND CIVILIANS WHO ARE GOING IN TO EVACUATE THE WOUNDED AND THE DEAD.

A MAJOR FLASHPOINT BETWEEN RUSSIA AND THE WEST IS THE CHARGE THAT RUSSIA PERMITTED AND COVERED UP THE SYRIAN MILITARY'S USE OF CHEMICAL WEAPONS ON CIVILIANS

RESEARCHERS FROM THE GLOBAL PUBLIC POLICY INSTITUTE (GPPI) IN BERLIN, ALONG WITH SYRIAN AND INTERNATIONAL PARTNERS, COMPILED 345 CREDIBLY SUBSTANTIATED OR CONFIRMED CHEMICAL WEAPON ATTACKS SINCE 2011 — BUILDING ON YEARS OF PAINSTAKING RESEARCH.

THE GPPI FOUND THAT APPROXIMATELY 98 PER CENT OF THE ATTACKS WERE CARRIED OUT BY THE ASSAD REGIME, USUALLY DROPPED FROM THE AIR, AND ISLAMIC STATE WERE RESPONSIBLE FOR THE REST.

ACCORDING TO THE GPPI RESEARCH, ASSAD'S USE OF CHLORINE BOMBS, IN PARTICULAR, IS A CRUCIAL PART OF THE REGIME'S MILITARY STRATEGY.

FIRST, CONVENTIONAL BOMBING DRIVES CIVILIANS INTO UNDERGROUND TUNNELS AND BASEMENTS...

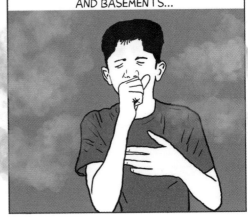

...THEN CHLORINE GAS, WHICH IS HEAVIER THAN AIR, SINKS INTO THESE LAST REFUGES; THE PEOPLE ARE FORCED TO FLEE THEIR HOMES AND TOWNS.

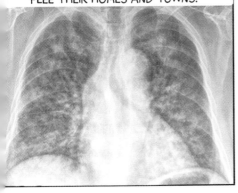

TOBIAS SCHNEIDER, A GPPI RESEARCH FELLOW, SAID...

OUR RESEARCH SHOWS WHAT SYRIANS ON THE GROUND HAVE KNOWN FOR YEARS: THAT CHEMICAL WEAPONS HAVE BECOME A COMPLETELY NORMALISED COMPONENT OF THE SYRIAN REGIME ARSENAL...

...USED FOR YEARS IN FULL VIEW OF THE INTERNATIONAL COMMUNITY WITH NEAR IMPUNITY.

RUSSIAN TROLLS AND DISINFORMATION OUTLETS WERE PIVOTAL IN SPREADING LIES ABOUT ASSAD'S WAR CRIMES IN SYRIA.

THEY CAST DOUBT ON INDEPENDENT INQUIRIES INTO THE REGIME'S USE OF CHEMICAL WEAPONS AGAINST CIVILIANS.

TROLLS AND RUSSIAN MEDIA OUTLETS ALSO CREATED NARRATIVES TARGETING RESCUE WORKERS, SUCH AS THE 'WHITE HELMETS', WITH BASELESS ACCUSATIONS THAT THEY STAGE ATTACKS OR ARE IN LEAGUE WITH TERRORIST GROUPS.

A 2018 REPORT BY THE ATLANTIC COUNCIL READ: 'RUSSIAN ACTIVE MEASURES FIRST FOCUSED ON CREATING AN ALTERNATE NARRATIVE ABOUT THE SYRIAN REVOLUTION TO INFLUENCE WESTERN POLICIES TOWARD DAMASCUS AND SOW CONFUSION IN WESTERN SOCIETIES.'

THE REPORT CITES A 2015 US STATE DEPARTMENT STUDY, WHICH ESTIMATES THAT RUSSIA INVESTS $1.4 BILLION A YEAR ON PROPAGANDA AND THINK TANK FUNDING, TO ADVANCE ITS DOMESTIC AND FOREIGN POLICY OBJECTIVES.

ANOTHER ATLANTIC COUNCIL PAPER QUOTES RUSSIAN GENERAL ALEKSANDR DVORNIKOV ON THE IMPORTANCE OF INFORMATION WARFARE.

I WILL SAY THIS: WITHOUT CARRYING OUT INFORMATION OPERATIONS, WE WOULD NOT HAVE HAD SUCCESS IN ALEPPO, DEIR AL-ZOUR AND GHOUTA.

THEY DID THIS BY 'GAMING' THE SOCIAL MEDIA ALGORITHMS WITH A FLOOD OF CONTENT BY PRO-ASSAD BLOGGERS, ALT-RIGHT MEDIA FIGURES AND SELF-DESCRIBED ANTI-IMPERIALISTS, BOOSTED BY A NETWORK OF AGITATORS.

IN THIS WAY, RUSSIAN PROPAGANDISTS WERE ABLE TO CREATE A 'MANUFACTURED CONSENSUS' THAT GAVE LEGITIMACY TO FRINGE VIEWS AND CONSPIRACY THEORIES.

TRUTH

DAVID PATRIKARAKOS, AUTHOR OF WAR IN 140 CHARACTERS: HOW SOCIAL MEDIA IS RESHAPING CONFLICT IN THE 21ST CENTURY, HAS SAID THAT...

THESE ARE TECHNIQUES THAT ARE THE HEART OF RUSSIAN PROPAGANDA.

THE OLD SOVIET UNION, PATRIKARAKOS POINTS OUT, WOULD PORTRAY THEIR COUNTRY AS A MODEL SOCIETY...

...BUT MODERN RUSSIA'S APPROACH IS TO CONFUSE EVERY ISSUE WITH SO MANY NARRATIVES THAT PEOPLE CAN'T RECOGNISE THE TRUTH WHEN THEY SEE IT.

WHY WAS RUSSIA FIGHTING IN SYRIA? WHAT WERE PUTIN'S AIMS?

MARGOT LIGHT, PROFESSOR EMERITUS IN INTERNATIONAL RELATIONS AT THE LONDON SCHOOL OF ECONOMICS, SAID THAT THE RUSSIANS NEVER CONSIDERED THE INTERESTS OF SYRIA, ONLY THEIR OWN

SHE DOESN'T THINK, SHE SAYS, THAT THE RUSSIANS HAVE ANY REAL BELIEF IN ASSAD. PART OF THEIR MOTIVATION IN BEING INVOLVED IN THE MIDDLE EAST IS SO THEY HAVE A SAY IN WORLD EVENTS.

IN ORDER TO BROKER A PEACE DEAL IN THE SYIAN CONFLICT, RUSSIA WOULD HAVE TO BE CONSULTED.

PUTIN IS DETERMINED TO SHOW THAT RUSSIA IS A STRONG POWER THAT HAS TO BE RECKONED WITH.

BUT ALSO, THE MIDDLE EAST IS CLOSER TO RUSSIA THAN IT IS TO THE UK OR US, SO THEY CONSIDER UNREST IN THE REGION A SECURITY THREAT.

NOVEMBER 2016.

DONALD TRUMP WAS ELECTED PRESIDENT OF THE UNITED STATES, BEATING DEMOCRATIC PARTY RIVAL HILLARY CLINTON.

US AUTHORITIES DETERMINED RUSSIA TRIED TO INTERFERE IN THE ELECTION IN TRUMP'S FAVOUR.

ON 19 MARCH 2016, HILLARY CLINTON'S CAMPAIGN CHAIRMAN JOHN PODESTA RECEIVED AN EMAIL CLAIMING TO BE AN ALERT FROM GOOGLE, SAYING THAT ANOTHER USER HAD TRIED TO ACCESS HIS ACCOUNT.

IT CONTAINED A LINK TO A PAGE WHERE PODESTA COULD CHANGE HIS PASSWORD. HE SHARED THE EMAIL WITH A STAFFER FROM THE CAMPAIGN'S HELP DESK, ASKING IF THE EMAIL WAS LEGITIMATE?

THE STAFFER'S REPLY CONTAINED A TYPO. INSTEAD OF TYPING *THIS IS AN ILLEGITIMATE EMAIL*, THE STAFFER TYPED *THIS IS A LEGITIMATE EMAIL*. PODESTA FOLLOWED THE INSTRUCTIONS AND TYPED A NEW PASSWORD, ALLOWING HACKERS TO GRAB HIS EMAILS.

APRIL 2016. HACKERS USED THE STOLEN CREDENTIALS TO ACCESS THE DEMOCRATIC CONGRESSIONAL CAMPAIGN COMMITTEE COMPUTER NETWORK, STEALING DATA WITH MALWARE.

12 JUNE 2016 — WIKILEAKS FOUNDER, JULIAN ASSANGE, SAID IN AN INTERVIEW THAT THE WEBSITE HAD OBTAINED AND WOULD PUBLISH A BATCH OF CAMPAIGN EMAILS.

15 JUNE 2016 — CROWDSTRIKE, A CYBERSECURITY FIRM HIRED BY THE DEMOCRATIC PARTY, POSTED A PUBLIC NOTICE ON ITS WEBSITE...

...DESCRIBING AN ATTACK ON THE POLITICAL COMMITTEE'S COMPUTER NETWORK BY TWO GROUPS ASSOCIATED WITH RUSSIAN INTELLIGENCE...

...CALLED 'COZY BEAR' AND 'FANCY BEAR'. THE GROUPS HAD TUNNELLED INTO THE COMMITTEE'S COMPUTER SYSTEM...

...AND SO THE HACKERS CREATED A PERSONA CALLED 'GUCCIFER 2.0', A SELF-DESCRIBED ROMANIAN BLOGGER WHO CLAIMED THAT HE ALONE CONDUCTED THE THEFT.

22 JULY 2016 — DAYS BEFORE THE DEMOCRATIC NATIONAL CONVENTION, WIKILEAKS PUBLISHED NEARLY 20,000 EMAILS HACKED FROM THE DNC SERVER.

THE DOCUMENTS INCLUDED NOTES FROM DEMOCRATIC NATIONAL COMMITTEE CHAIR, DEBBIE WASSERMAN SCHULTZ, INSULTING STAFFERS FROM THE BERNIE SANDERS CAMPAIGN — CLINTON'S RIVAL TO BE THE DEMOCRATIC PRESIDENTIAL NOMINEE...

...AS WELL AS MESSAGES THAT SUGGESTED THE DNC WAS FAVOURING CLINTON RATHER THAN REMAINING NEUTRAL. WASSERMAN SCHULTZ RESIGNED AS CHAIR SOON AFTER.

OTHER EMAILS THAT WIKILEAKS RELEASED INCLUDED EXCERPTS FROM SPEECHES THAT CLINTON HAD GIVEN TO BANKS, REGARDING HIGH FEES — WHICH SHE HAD REFUSED TO RELEASE DURING THE CAMPAIGN.

THESE SPEECHES WERE USED BY DETRACTORS TO SHOW THAT, DESPITE HER LIBERAL RHETORIC, CLINTON WAS IN THE POCKET OF WALL STREET.

25 JULY 2016 — THE FBI ANNOUNCED IT HAD LAUNCHED AN INVESTIGATION INTO THE HACK. OFFICIALS TOLD THE MEDIA THEY THOUGHT THE CYBERATTACK WAS LINKED TO RUSSIA.

27 JULY 2016 — DURING A PRESS CONFERENCE, TRUMP TALKED ABOUT CLINTON'S USE OF A PRIVATE EMAIL SERVER AND CALLED ON HACKERS TO FIND DELETED EMAILS.

RUSSIA, IF YOU'RE LISTENING, I HOPE YOU'RE ABLE TO FIND THE 30,000 EMAILS THAT ARE MISSING.

7 OCTOBER 2016 — THE DEPARTMENT OF HOMELAND SECURITY AND THE OFFICE OF NATIONAL INTELLIGENCE ON ELECTION SECURITY ISSUED A STATEMENT DECLARING THAT THE INTELLIGENCE COMMUNITY WAS...

CONFIDENT THAT THE RUSSIAN GOVERNMENT DIRECTED THE RECENT COMPROMISES OF EMAILS FROM US PERSONS AND INSTITUTIONS.

29 DECEMBER 2016 — IN ONE OF HIS LAST ACTS BEFORE LEAVING OFFICE, OBAMA ISSUED AN EXECUTIVE ORDER WITH SANCTIONS AGAINST RUSSIA — NAMING SIX RUSSIANS WHO TOOK PART IN THE HACKING. ADDITIONALLY, 35 RUSSIAN DIPLOMATS WERE ORDERED TO LEAVE THE UNITED STATES.

3 JANUARY 2017 — DURING AN INTERVIEW WITH FOX NEWS, ASSANGE SAID THAT THE RUSSIAN GOVERNMENT DID NOT PROVIDE HIM WITH THE HACKED DNC EMAILS.

17 MAY 2017 — THE US DEPUTY ATTORNEY GENERAL ROD ROSENSTEIN APPOINTED FORMER FBI DIRECTOR ROBERT MUELLER AS SPECIAL COUNSEL TO LEAD AN INVESTIGATION INTO RUSSIAN INTERFERENCE.

ONE OF THE INCIDENTS MUELLER WAS TASKED TO INVESTIGATE HAPPENED ON 9 JUNE 2016: WHEN DONALD TRUMP'S SON, DONALD TRUMP JR...

...CAMPAIGN MANAGER PAUL MANAFORT...

...AND TRUMP'S SON-IN-LAW, JARED KUSHNER...

...SECRETLY MET WITH A RUSSIAN LAWYER IN TRUMP TOWER IN NEW YORK.

THE PERSON WHO HELPED SET UP THE MEETING, ROB GOLDSTONE, TOLD TRUMP JUNIOR IN AN EMAIL THAT...

...THE RUSSIAN GOVERNMENT WANTED TO PROVIDE HIM DAMAGING INFORMATION ON HILLARY CLINTON TO HELP HIS FATHER'S ELECTION CAMPAIGN.

IN EXCHANGE TRUMP JUNIOR SUGGESTED THE POSSIBILITY OF MORE FAVOURABLE TREATMENT FOR RUSSIA UNDER THE TRUMP ADMINISTRATION.

SHORTLY AFTER THE MEETING, TRUMP JR MADE A CALL TO A BLOCKED PHONE NUMBER. IT IS KNOWN THAT HIS FATHER HAS A BLOCKED PHONE NUMBER.

IN THE EVENTUAL REPORT, WHICH WAS SUBMITTED ON 22 MARCH 2019, MUELLER STATED THAT THIS MEETING DID NOT AMOUNT TO A CRIMINAL OFFENCE...

...IN PART, BECAUSE THE INVESTIGATING TEAM WAS UNABLE TO ESTABLISH THAT THE PARTICIPANTS KNEW THAT THEIR CONDUCT WAS ILLEGAL.

OH YEAH?

MUELLER WAS ALSO UNABLE TO CONCLUDE THAT THE INFORMATION WAS A 'THING OF VALUE' EXCEEDING $25,000, THE REQUIREMENT FOR CAMPAIGN FINANCE TO BE A FELONY, AS OPPOSED TO MERELY A CIVIL VIOLATION OF LAW.

REALLY?

THE REPORT WENT ON TO STATE THAT ALTHOUGH THIS CONDUCT DID NOT TECHNICALLY AMOUNT TO CONSPIRACY THAT DID NOT MEAN IT WAS ACCEPTABLE.

IT ISN'T.

THE TRUMP CAMPAIGN MEMBERS CLEARLY WELCOMED FOREIGN INFLUENCE INTO THE ELECTION AND THEN COMPROMISED THEMSELVES BY COVERING IT UP.

YOU DON'T SAY.

THIS WASN'T THE ONLY CONTACT WITH RUSSIA THAT MUELLER FOUND – OTHER COMMUNICATION INCLUDED THE SHARING OF POLLING DATA ABOUT MIDWESTERN STATES WHERE TRUMP LATER WON VICTORIES...

..AND CONTACT WITH WIKILEAKS AFTER IT HAD RECEIVED EMAILS STOLEN BY RUSSIA.

WHILE NONE OF THESE ACTS AMOUNTED TO THE CRIME OF CONSPIRACY, MUELLER CONCLUDED, IT COULD BE DESCRIBED AS 'COLLUSION.'

IT CERTAINLY SEEMS LIKE A CONSPIRACY TO ME

HOW CAN MUELLER SAY IT ISN'T?

A SENIOR MEMBER OF ROBERT MUELLER'S TEAM, ANDREW WEISSMANN, WAS EVENTUALLY TO WRITE THAT THE SPECIAL COUNSEL WAS TOO TIMID IN HIS INVESTIGATION OF DONALD TRUMP AND HIS LINKS TO MOSCOW.

WEISSMANN SAID MUELLER AND HIS TOP DEPUTY, AARON ZEBLEY, AVOIDED STEPS THAT WOULD LEAD TO CONFRONTATION WITH THE WHITE HOUSE...

ACCORDING TO WEISSMANN, ANYTIME THE INQUIRY REACHED A CRITICAL JUNCTURE, ZEBLEY WOULD SAY THEY COULD NOT TAKE THAT PARTICULAR ACTION, FOR FEAR IT WOULD AGGRAVATE THE PRESIDENT.

WEISSMANN SAID MUELLER WAS AFRAID OF BEING FIRED.

THAT'S PATHETIC. THIS INVESTIGATION WAS THEIR JOB. WHY WERE THEY SO TIMID?

HE FELT THAT IF THEY HAD USED ALL THE MEANS AT THEIR DISPOSAL TO UNCOVER THE TRUTH, REGARDLESS OF THE PRESIDENT'S EFFORTS TO UNDERMINE THE INQUIRY...

...THEY WOULD HAVE ACHIEVED FAR MORE.

NOT ONLY DID TRUMP DENY COLLUSION WITH RUSSIA, HE DEFENDED PUTIN WHENEVER HE COULD.

EVERY TIME HE [PUTIN] SEES ME, HE SAYS, 'I DIDN'T DO THAT.' AND I BELIEVE — I REALLY BELIEVE — THAT WHEN HE TELLS ME THAT, HE MEANS IT.

THE MUELLER INVESTIGATION INDICTED 34 PEOPLE: SEVEN US NATIONALS, 26 RUSSIAN NATIONALS, ONE DUTCH NATIONAL AND THREE RUSSIAN ORGANISATIONS.

FORMER TRUMP CAMPAIGN CHAIRMAN PAUL MANAFORT FACED CHARGES IN TWO SEPARATE FEDERAL COURTS – A SLEW OF FINANCIAL CRIME CHARGES RELATED LARGELY TO HIS LOBBYING WORK IN UKRAINE...

...SENTENCED TO SEVEN AND A HALF YEARS IN PRISON.

RICK GATES, A FORMER TRUMP CAMPAIGN OFFICIAL, WAS CHARGED IN CONNECTION TO FINANCIAL CRIMES, UNREGISTERED FOREIGN LOBBYING AND ON ALLEGATIONS THAT HE MADE FALSE STATEMENTS TO FEDERAL PROSECUTORS...

...SENTENCED TO 45 DAYS IN JAIL AND THREE YEARS PROBATION.

MICHAEL COHEN, TRUMP'S FORMER PERSONAL ATTORNEY AND LONG-TIME FIXER, PLEADED GUILTY TO ONE COUNT OF MAKING FALSE STATEMENTS TO CONGRESS...

...SENTENCED TO THREE YEARS IN PRISON.

LT GENERAL MICHAEL FLYNN, WHO HAD SERVED AS TRUMP'S NATIONAL SECURITY ADVISER, PLEADED GUILTY TO MAKING FALSE STATEMENTS TO THE FBI ABOUT HIS INTERACTIONS WITH THE RUSSIAN AMBASSADOR...

...PARDONED BY PRESIDENT TRUMP.

GEORGE PAPADOPOULOS, A TRUMP CAMPAIGN ADVISER, PLEADED GUILTY TO LYING TO THE FBI ABOUT THE TIMING OF MEETINGS WITH GO-BETWEENS FOR RUSSIA.

SENTENCED TO 14 DAYS INCARCERATION. PARDONED BY PRESIDENT TRUMP.

ALEX VAN DER ZWAAN, A DUTCH LAWYER WHO LIED TO THE FBI ABOUT HIS CONTACTS WITH RICK GATES, AND A PERSON THE FBI ASSESSED AS BEING TIED TO RUSSIAN MILITARY INTELLIGENCE...

...RECEIVED 30 DAYS IN PRISON. PARDONED BY DONALD TRUMP.

RICHARD PINEDO, A CALIFORNIA COMPUTER EXPERT CAUGHT SELLING FAKE ONLINE IDENTITIES TO RUSSIANS, WAS SENTENCED TO SIX MONTHS IN PRISON.

ROGER STONE, A LONG-TIME TRUMP ADVISOR, WAS SENTENCED TO 40 MONTHS IN PRISON FOR MAKING FALSE STATEMENTS, WITNESS TAMPERING AND OBSTRUCTION OF JUSTICE.

PARDONED BY DONALD TRUMP.

UKRAINIAN BUSINESSMAN KONSTANTIN KILIMNIK, WHO WORKED FOR TRUMP CAMPAIGN CHAIRMAN PAUL MANAFORT, AND IS TIED TO RUSSIAN INTELLIGENCE, WAS CHARGED WITH CONSPIRACY TO OBSTRUCT JUSTICE.

HE REMAINS OUTSIDE OF THE REACH OF US LAW ENFORCEMENT. THE FBI ARE OFFERING A $250,000 REWARD FOR INFORMATION LEADING TO HIS ARREST.

WITH THESE PARDONS TRUMP CONCLUDED A FOUR-YEAR CAMPAIGN TO COVER UP HIS OWN WRONGDOING IN THE RUSSIAGATE SCANDAL.

TRUMP AIDED AND ABETTED VLADIMIR PUTIN'S ATTACK ON THE 2016 ELECTION, WHICH HAD THE AIM OF HELPING TRUMP WIN THE WHITE HOUSE.

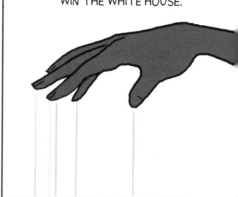

THERE IS NO KNOWN EXPLANATION FOR TRUMP'S CEASELESS FEALTY TO PUTIN, OR HIS INABILITY TO CRITICISE THE DICTATOR, NO MATTER WHAT EVIL ACT THE RUSSIAN STATE COMMITTED UNDER PUTIN'S DIRECTION.

ONLY TIME WILL REVEAL THE TRUE REASON FOR TRUMP'S INABILITY TO ACT IN THE UNITED STATES' BEST INTERESTS.

THIS PRESIDENT HAS BEEN THE MOST EXTRAORDINARY GIFT TO THE KREMLIN.

ADAM SCHIFF

CHAIRMAN OF THE HOUSE INTELLIGENCE COMMITTEE

ACROSS EVERY FIELD, IN TERMS OF AMERICA'S STANDING IN THE WORLD, IN TERMS OF AMERICA'S COHESION AT HOME...

...NO PRESIDENT HAS DONE MORE TO DAMAGE THE UNITED STATES OR TO ADVANTAGE THE KREMLIN THAN DONALD TRUMP. THAT WILL BE HIS LASTING LEGACY.

UNDER PRESIDENT TRUMP, THE US ABANDONED INTERNATIONAL CLIMATE AND NUCLEAR ARMS AGREEMENTS...

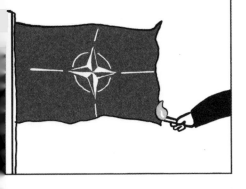

...IT ANNOUNCED ITS WITHDRAWAL FROM THE WORLD HEALTH ORGANISATION, QUESTIONED THE FUTURE OF NATO...

...AND ANTAGONISED ALLIES LIKE GERMANY.

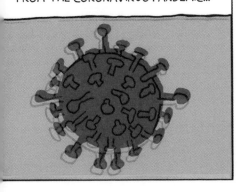

AMERICA'S MORAL AUTHORITY WAS ALSO UNDERCUT BY THE HIGH DEATH TOLL AND ECONOMIC FALLOUT FROM THE CORONAVIRUS PANDEMIC...

...COUPLED WITH THE RACIAL RECKONING THAT CONVULSED THE COUNTRY.

THESE HIGHLIGHTS FROM TRUMP'S FOUR YEARS IN OFFICE READ LIKE PUTIN'S WISH LIST. FEW COUNTRIES HAVE BENEFITED MORE GEOPOLITICALLY FROM TRUMP'S TIME IN OFFICE THAN RUSSIA.

SOME EXAMPLES OF TRUMP'S DEFERENCE TO PUTIN: HE SUGGESTED RUSSIA COULD KEEP CRIMEA. HE BROKE WITH US POLICY AND SAID HE WAS OK IF RUSSIA KEPT THE UKRAINIAN TERRITORY.

HE REPEATED A KREMLIN TALKING POINT, SAYING...

THE PEOPLE OF CRIMEA, FROM WHAT I'VE HEARD, WOULD RATHER BE WITH RUSSIA THAN WHERE THEY WERE.

TRUMP ANNOUNCED IN OCTOBER 2019 THAT US TROOPS WERE WITHDRAWING FROM NORTHERN SYRIA. TRUMP'S SYRIA WITHDRAWAL GAVE PUTIN A BOOST.

THE ABRUPT MOVE CLEARED THE WAY FOR TURKEY TO CONQUER TERRITORIES PREVIOUSLY CONTROLLED BY THE US AND ALLIED KURDISH MILITIAS.

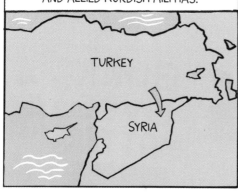

IT ALSO GAVE RUSSIA A GOLDEN OPPORTUNITY TO EXPAND ITS INFLUENCE AND SWIFTLY TAKE OVER ABANDONED US OUTPOSTS AND CHECKPOINTS.

TRUMP REFUSED TO SAY PUTIN WAS A KILLER AND DISMISSED CREDIBLE ALLEGATIONS THAT HE ASSASSINATED HIS OPPONENTS.

TRUMP SAID IN 2015...

I THINK IT WOULD BE DESPICABLE IF THAT TOOK PLACE, BUT I HAVEN'T SEEN ANY EVIDENCE THAT HE KILLED ANYBODY.

THE PRESIDENT WAS REPEATEDLY TOLD DURING IN-PERSON BRIEFINGS AND IN WRITTEN INTELLIGENCE REPORTS IN 2019 AND 2020 THAT THE US GOVERNMENT BELIEVED RUSSIA PAID BOUNTIES TO AFGHAN MILITANTS TO KILL US SOLDIERS.

DESPITE BEING GIVEN THIS INFORMATION, TRUMP DID NOT PUBLICLY CONDEMN RUSSIA OR TAKE ANY RETALIATORY ACTIONS.

DONALD TRUMP ALSO DISPUTED THAT RUSSIA WAS BEHIND THE ATTEMPTED MURDER OF FORMER RUSSIAN SPY SERGEI SKRIPAL IN 2018.

A YEAR AFTER THE ATTACK, IN A TENSE CALL WITH THE BRITISH PRIME MINISTER THERESA MAY, TRUMP IS SAID TO HAVE SPENT TEN MINUTES EXPRESSING HIS DOUBTS ABOUT RUSSIAN INVOLVEMENT.

ON 4 MARCH 2018, SERGEI SKRIPAL — A FORMER OFFICER WITH RUSSIA'S GRU MILITARY INTELLIGENCE AGENCY AND DOUBLE AGENT FOR THE BRITISH INTELLIGENCE AGENCIES — AND HIS DAUGHTER, YULIA SKRIPAL, WERE FOUND UNCONSCIOUS ON A PARK BENCH IN THE CITY OF SALISBURY, ENGLAND.

THEY WERE POISONED WITH A MILITARY-GRADE NERVE AGENT OF A TYPE DEVELOPED BY RUSSIA, KNOWN AS NOVICHOK, WHICH EARLIER THAT DAY HAD BEEN SPRAYED ON THE DOOR HANDLE OF THEIR HOME.

ALSO EXPOSED TO THE NOVICHOK WAS DETECTIVE SERGEANT NICK BAILEY, WHO WAS LEFT IN CRITICAL CARE WHEN INVESTIGATING THE SKRIPAL POISONINGS.

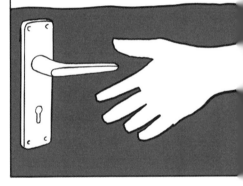

IT SOUNDS FOOLISH, BUT I PUT IT DOWN TO EXHAUSTION AND MIGRAINES BECAUSE, AT THAT TIME, WE HAD NO IDEA WHAT WE WERE DEALING WITH.

TAKEN SERIOUSLY ILL, HE WAS IN AN INTENSIVE CARE UNIT FOR THREE WEEKS.

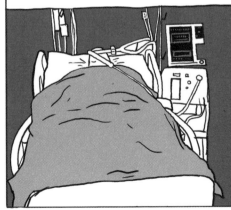

THE NOVICHOK WAS SPRAYED FROM A CONVERTED PERFUME BOTTLE AND THEN DISCARDED IN A SKIP.

A LOCAL MAN, CHARLIE ROWLEY, FOUND THE BOTTLE. HE FELL ILL, BUT SURVIVED.

UNFORTUNATELY, THE WOMAN HE GAVE THE BOTTLE TO, DAWN STURGESS, SPRAYED IT ON HER WRIST. SHE DIED IN HOSPITAL.

DAWN STURGESS WAS THE ONLY PERSON TO DIE IN THE SALISBURY ATTACK. BOTH THE INTENDED VICTIM, SERGEI SKRIPAL AND HIS DAUGHTER, YULIA, SURVIVED.

POLICE SIFTED THROUGH THOUSANDS OF HOURS OF CCTV FOOTAGE.

THEY IDENTIFIED THE BUNGLING ASSASSINS AS TWO RUSSIAN MEN — RUSLAN BOSHIROV AND ALEXANDER PETROV — WHO VISITED SALISBURY DURING THAT WEEKEND, NOT ONCE BUT TWICE.

THE PAIR HAD FLOWN IN FROM MOSCOW TO GATWICK AIRPORT WITH RUSSIAN PASSPORTS AND VISAS. THE SUSPICION WAS THAT THEY WERE UNDERCOVER OPERATIVES TRAVELLING UNDER ASSUMED NAMES.

THEY WERE RECORDED ARRIVING AT SALISBURY TRAIN STATION, WALKING IN THE DIRECTION OF SKRIPAL'S HOME AND RETURNING AFTERWARDS — VISIBLY RELIEVED, WITH PETROV GRINNING.

BACK IN MOSCOW, THE PAIR APPEARED ON RUSSIAN STATE TV. PETROV SAID FRIENDS HAD SUGGESTED THEY VISIT SALISBURY — A 'WONDERFUL CITY'. BOSHIROV ADDED THAT THEY WERE ATTRACTED BY THE CITY'S CATHEDRAL AND SPIRE. IT WAS AN UNINTENTIONALLY COMIC PERFORMANCE THAT LED TO WIDESPREAD ONLINE MOCKERY.

THE INVESTIGATIVE WEBSITE BELLINGCAT EVENTUALLY IDENTIFIED RUSLAN BOSHIROV AS THE HIGHLY DECORATED GRU COLONEL ANATOLIY CHEPIGA...

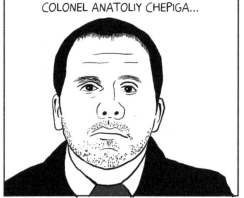

...AND ALEXANDER PETROV AS DR ALEXANDER MISHKIN, ALSO OF THE GRU.

PRIME MINISTER THERESA MAY UNVEILED A SERIES OF MEASURES ON 14 MARCH 2018 IN RETALIATION FOR THE NERVE AGENT ATTACK, AFTER THE RUSSIAN GOVERNMENT REFUSED TO MEET THE UK'S REQUEST FOR AN EXPLANATION OF THE INCIDENT.

THIS INCLUDED THE EXPULSION OF 23 RUSSIAN DIPLOMATS WHICH SHE PRESENTED AS 'ACTIONS TO DISMANTLE THE RUSSIAN ESPIONAGE NETWORK IN THE UK', AS THESE DIPLOMATS HAD BEEN IDENTIFIED BY THE UK AS 'UNDECLARED INTELLIGENCE AGENTS'.

MORE THAN 20 WESTERN COUNTRIES EXPELLED RUSSIAN DIPLOMATS IN SOLIDARITY WITH THE UK. ABOUT 150 EMBASSY-BASED SPIES, MOSTLY GRU OFFICERS, WERE FORCED TO PACK THEIR BAGS.

DESPITE PRESIDENT TRUMP'S UNWILLINGNESS TO ACCEPT THAT THE SALISBURY POISONINGS WERE A RUSSIAN OPERATION, THE BIGGEST CLEAROUT OF RUSSIAN SPIES TOOK PLACE IN THE US.

THE TRUMP ADMINISTRATION REMOVED 60 RUSSIAN OFFICIALS, INCLUDING A DOZEN BASED AT THE UN IN NEW YORK...

...AND SHUT THE CONSULATE IN SEATTLE, ENDING THE RUSSIAN FEDERATION'S DIPLOMATIC REPRESENTATION ON THE US WEST COAST. WAS THIS A SIGN THAT TRUMP WAS FINALLY GETTING TOUGH ON RUSSIA? IT WOULD SEEM NOT. ACCORDING TO TRUMP'S NATIONAL SECURITY ADVISER, JOHN BOLTON, AFTER THE SANCTIONS WERE ANNOUNCED, TRUMP TRIED TO RESCIND THEM AND THOUGHT THE US WAS...

BEING TOO TOUGH ON PUTIN.

YURI SHVETS, A KGB MAJOR WHO HAD A COVER JOB AS A CORRESPONDENT IN WASHINGTON FOR THE RUSSIAN NEWS AGENCY TASS DURING THE 1980S, HAS NO DOUBT THAT DONALD TRUMP WAS CULTIVATED AS A RUSSIAN ASSET.

THIS IS AN EXAMPLE WHERE PEOPLE WERE RECRUITED WHEN THEY WERE JUST STUDENTS AND THEN THEY ROSE TO IMPORTANT POSITIONS; SOMETHING LIKE THAT WAS HAPPENING WITH TRUMP.

CRAIG UNGER, THE AUTHOR OF *HOUSE OF TRUMP, HOUSE OF PUTIN*, AND *AMERICAN KOMPROMAT: HOW THE KGB CULTIVATED DONALD TRUMP, AND RELATED TALES OF SEX, GREED, POWER, AND TREACHERY*, SAID OF TRUMP:

HE WAS AN ASSET. IT WAS NOT THIS GRAND, INGENIOUS PLAN THAT WE'RE GOING TO DEVELOP THIS GUY AND 40 YEARS LATER HE'LL BE PRESIDENT. AT THE TIME IT STARTED, WHICH WAS AROUND 1980, THE RUSSIANS WERE TRYING TO RECRUIT LIKE CRAZY AND GOING AFTER DOZENS AND DOZENS OF PEOPLE.

TRUMP WAS THE PERFECT TARGET IN A LOT OF WAYS: HIS VANITY, NARCISSISM, MADE HIM A NATURAL TARGET TO RECRUIT. HE WAS CULTIVATED OVER A 40-YEAR PERIOD, RIGHT UP THROUGH HIS ELECTION.

MEANWHILE, IN RUSSIA, ON 7 MAY 2018 VLADIMIR PUTIN BEGAN HIS FOURTH TERM AS PRESIDENT OF RUSSIA. HE ONCE AGAIN INVITED DMITRY MEDVEDEV TO FORM A GOVERNMENT.

2018

TWO YEARS LATER, IN JANUARY 2020, PUTIN'S ENTIRE CABINET, INCLUDING PRIME MINISTER DMITRY MEDVEDEV, ABRUPTLY RESIGNED IN A MOVE AIMED AT EASING PROPOSED CONSTITUTIONAL CHANGES.

THESE CHANGES INCLUDED REFORMS THAT WOULD RESET PUTIN'S TERM COUNT TO ZERO, ALLOWING HIM TO SERVE TWO MORE SIX-YEAR TERMS, ENABLING HIM TO REMAIN PRESIDENT UNTIL 2036.

I'LL BE 83 THEN

A RAFT OF OTHER REFORMS INCLUDED THE OUTLAWING OF SAME-SEX MARRIAGE, A PROCLAMATION OF A BELIEF IN GOD, AND AN ATTEMPT AT PREVENTING ANY FUTURE LEGISLATON THAT WOULD END RUSSIA'S ILLEGAL OCCUPATION OF CRIMEA.

CRIMEA

EX-PRIME MINISTER MEDVEDEV WAS DEMOTED TO DEPUTY OF THE NATIONAL SECURITY COUNCIL.

FOR THE NEW PRIME MINISTER, PUTIN NOMINATED MIKHAIL MISHUSTIN, WHO HAD BEEN HEAD OF THE COUNTRY'S FEDERAL TAX SERVICE.

THE REFERENDUM ON THE CONSTITUTIONAL CHANGES WAS HELD BETWEEN 25 JUNE AND 1 JULY 2020. NEARLY 78 PER CENT OF RUSSIAN VOTERS BACKED PUTIN'S CONSOLIDATION OF POWER.

GOLOS, AN INDEPENDENT RUSSIAN ELECTI[ON] MONITORING GROUP, HAS ALLEGED THER[E] WERE MANY VIOLATIONS OF DEMOCRACY

GOLOS, MEANING 'VOTE' OR 'VOICE'.

AMONG ITS CRITICISMS: OPPONENTS WERE BARRED FROM CAMPAIGNING IN THE MEDIA; REMOTE ELECTRONIC VOTING WAS ORGANISED ON AN ILLEGAL BASIS AND ELECTION MONITORS WERE APPOINTED BY A GOVERNMENT BODY.

GET RID OF THOSE VOTES.

THESE WEREN'T THE ONLY POLITICAL CHANGES THAT YEAR. IN DECEMBER, PUTI[N] SIGNED INTO LAW A BILL GRANTING RUSSIAN PRESIDENTS AND THEIR FAMILY MEMBERS *LIFETIME* IMMUNITY FROM CRIMINA[L] PROSECUTION.

THE LAW

UNDER THE NEW LAW, FORMER PRESIDENTS ARE IMMUNE FROM CRIMINAL OR ADMINISTRATIVE PROSECUTION AND MAY NOT BE DETAINED, ARRESTED OR SUBJECT TO SEARCHES OR INTERROGATIONS.

IN 2020, PUTIN WAS CLEARLY PREPARING THE WAY FOR HIS RETIREMENT AND ENSURING HIS SAFETY FROM WHOEVER FOLLOWS HIM AS PRESIDENT. HE WAS ALSO BUSY PROTECTING HIS HEALTH...

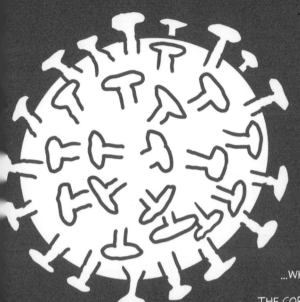

THEN CAME COVID

...WHILE THE COVID PANDEMIC
SWEPT THE WORLD.
THE CORONAVIRUS COVID-19, CAUSED
BY SEVERE ACUTE RESPIRATORY SYNDROME,
WAS FIRST IDENTIFIED IN DECEMBER 2019 IN
WUHAN, CHINA.

THE WORLD HEALTH ORGANISATION DECLARED THE OUTBREAK A
PUBLIC HEALTH EMERGENCY OF INTERNATIONAL CONCERN IN JANUARY
2020 AND A PANDEMIC IN MARCH 2020.

FOR MUCH OF THE PANDEMIC
PUTIN AND THE RUSSIAN
AUTHORITIES DOWNPLAYED
THE COUNTRY'S DEATH
TOLL. AS LATE AS DECEMBER
2020 IT WAS STILL BEING
CLAIMED BY THE KREMLIN
THAT FATALITIES WERE
AROUND 57,000.

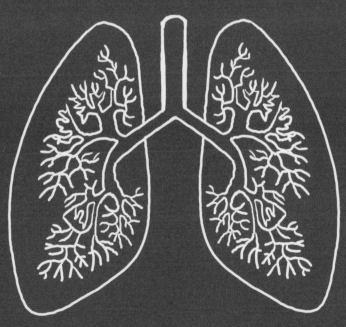

THESE CLAIMS OF AN EXTRAORDINARILY LOW
MORTALITY RATE WERE DISMISSED AS IMPLAUSIBLE
BY FOREIGN OBSERVERS AND RUSSIAN DOCTORS
ALIKE. EVERY OTHER INDICATOR, FROM PACKED
HOSPITALS WITH LONG LINES OF AMBULANCES
TO MORTALITY AMONG HEALTH WORKERS, PAINTED
A PICTURE OF A COUNTRY HIT HARD BY THE
PANDEMIC, NOT ONE MIRACULOUSLY SPARED.

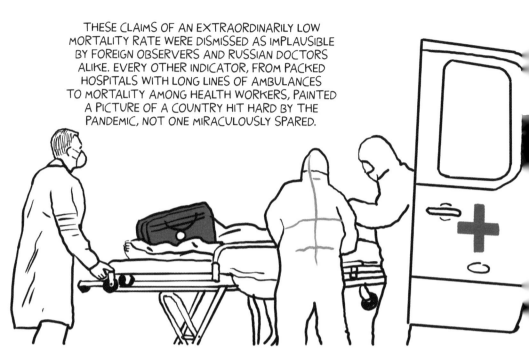

THE COUNTRY'S DEPUTY PRIME MINISTER FOR SOCIAL AFFAIRS, TATYANA GOLIKOVA, WOULD
EVENTUALLY CONCEDE, IN DECEMBER 2020, THAT THE TRUE DEATH TOLL WAS MORE THAN 180,00

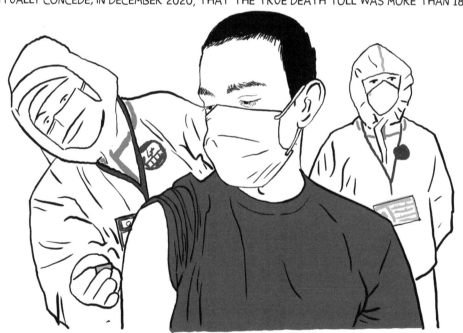

EMERGENCY MASS-DISTRIBUTION OF THE COVID-19 VACCINE, SPUTNIK V, BEGAN THAT MONTH.
THE VACCINE WAS INITIALLY MET WITH SOME CONTROVERSY AFTER
BEING ROLLED OUT BEFORE THE FINAL TRIAL DATA HAD BEEN RELEASED. BUT SPUTNIK V
GIVES AROUND 92 PER CENT PROTECTION AGAINST COVID-19, ACCORDING TO RESULTS
PUBLISHED IN THE UK MEDICAL JOURNAL *THE LANCET*.

TIN TOOK EVERY PRECAUTION TO AVOID THE VIRUS. HE SPENT MUCH OF 2020. CLUDED AT HIS DACHA OUTSIDE MOSCOW. SITORS HAD TO UNDERGO A TWO-WEEK QUARANTINE AND THEN WALK THROUGH A SPECIALLY BUILT CORRIDOR IN WHICH THEY WERE SPRAYED FROM ALL SIDES WITH DISINFECTANT.

THE RUSSIAN OPPOSITION LEADER, ALEXEI NAVALNY, MOCKED THE PRESIDENT'S ABUNDANCE OF CAUTION, REFERRING TO HIM AS...

GRANDPA IN HIS BUNKER.

NAVALNY IS A LAWYER WHO CAME TO TERNATIONAL PROMINENCE BY ORGANISING NTI-GOVERNMENT DEMONSTRATIONS AND RUNNING FOR OFFICE TO ADVOCATE EFORMS AGAINST CORRUPTION IN RUSSIA.

AS THE LEADER OF THE 'RUSSIA OF THE FUTURE PARTY', NAVALNY HAS BEEN DESCRIBED AS 'THE MAN VLADIMIR PUTIN FEARS MOST' BY THE WALL STREET JOURNAL.

NAVALNY IS OF RUSSIAN AND UKRAINIAN DESCENT. HE GREW UP IN OBNINSK ABOUT 62 MILES SOUTH-WEST OF MOSCOW, BUT SPENT HIS CHILDHOOD SUMMERS WITH HIS GRANDMOTHER IN UKRAINE, ACQUIRING PROFICIENCY IN THE UKRAINIAN LANGUAGE.

ПУТІНА — ГЕТЬ. *

* DOWN WITH PUTIN.

IN A 2011 RADIO INTERVIEW, HE DESCRIBED RUSSIA'S RULING PARTY, UNITED RUSSIA, AS A PARTY OF...

CROOKS AND THIEVES.

HE HAS BEEN JAILED MORE THAN TEN TIMES AND HAS SPENT HUNDREDS OF DAYS IN CUSTODY, CHARGED WITH SPURIOUS OR TRUMPED-UP CHARGES, SUCH AS, DEFYING A GOVERNMENT OFFICIAL, ORGANISING ILLEGAL DEMONSTRATIONS, AND EMBEZZLEMENT. BANNED FROM APPEARING ON STATE CONTROLLED TV, NAVALNY HAS HAD TO TAKE ANOTHER APPROACH TO REACH HIS AUDIENCE. HE HAS MORE THAN 6.5 MILLION YOUTUBE SUBSCRIBERS AND MORE THAN TWO MILLION TWITTER FOLLOWERS.

IN MARCH 2017, NAVALNY AND THE ANTI-CORRUPTION FOUNDATION (FBK) RELEASED THE DOCUMENTARY *HE IS NOT DIMON TO YOU* ON YOUTUBE, ACCUSING DMITRY MEDVEDEV, THE THEN PRIME MINISTER AND FORMER PRESIDENT OF RUSSIA, OF CORRUPTION.

THE FILM ESTIMATED THAT AS MUCH AS $1.2 BILLION HAD BEEN EMBEZZLED BY MEDVEDEV. THESE REVELATIONS LED TO MASS PROTESTS ACROSS THE COUNTRY.

OTHER INVESTIGATIONS ACCUSED FIRST DEPUTY PRIME MINISTER IGOR SHUVALOV OF CORRUPTION, STATING THAT COMPANIES OWNED BY BILLIONAIRES ROMAN ABRAMOVICH AND ALISHER USMANOV HAD TRANSFERRED TENS OF MILLIONS OF DOLLARS TO SHUVALOV'S COMPANY...

...ALLOWING SHUVALOV TO SHARE IN THE PROFIT FROM USMANOV'S PURCHASE OF THE BRITISH STEEL COMPANY CORUS.

corus

NAVALNY POSTED SCANS OF DOCUMENTS TO HIS BLOG SHOWING THE MONEY TRANSFERS. USMANOV AND SHUVALOV STATED THE DOCUMENTS NAVALNY HAD POSTED WERE LEGITIMATE, BUT THAT THE TRANSACTION HAD NOT VIOLATED RUSSIAN LAW.

I UNSWERVINGLY FOLLOWED THE RULES AND PRINCIPLES OF CONFLICT OF INTEREST. FOR A LAWYER, THIS IS SACRED.

NAVALNY ALSO ALLEGED THAT VIKTOR ZOLOTOV, THE DIRECTOR OF THE NATIONAL GUARD OF RUSSIA AND A MEMBER OF THE SECURITY COUNCIL OF RUSSIA, STOLE AT LEAST $29 MILLION FROM PROCUREMENT CONTRACTS FOR THE NATIONAL GUARD OF RUSSIA.

SUBSEQUENTLY, VIKTOR ZOLOTOV PUBLISHED A VIDEO MESSAGE CHALLENGING NAVALNY TO A DUEL.

I SIMPLY CHALLENGE YOU TO A DUEL, IN THE RING, ON THE JUDO MAT, ANYWHERE, AND I PROMISE TO MAKE MINCEMEAT OF YOU.

SUCH THREATS MIGHT SEEM LAUGHABLE, BUT AS WE HAVE SEEN, OPPONENTS OF PUTIN AND HIS CRIMINAL ASSOCIATES HAVE A TENDENCY TO EITHER BE GUNNED DOWN OR FALL MYSTERIOUSLY ILL IN WHAT IS NOW A FAMILIAR PATTERN.

ON 20 AUGUST 2020, NAVALNY BECAME CONFUSED AND BEGAN TO SWEAT HEAVILY WHILE RETURNING BY PLANE TO MOSCOW FROM THE SIBERIAN CITY OF TOMSK.

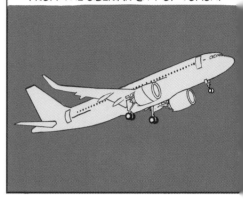

APPROXIMATELY 10 MINUTES AFTER DEPARTURE HE COLLAPSED, AND LOST CONSCIOUSNESS.

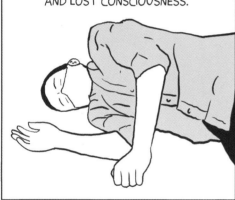

AFTER AN EMERGENCY LANDING, NAVALNY WAS ADMITTED TO THE TOXICOLOGY UNIT OF A LOCAL HOSPITAL IN OMSK.

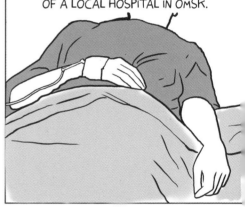

ON 22 AUGUST, NAVALNY WAS TRANSFERRED BY A GERMAN AIR AMBULANCE TO THE CHARITÉ HOSPITAL IN BERLIN AT THE REQUEST OF HIS FAMILY.

TESTS FROM MULTIPLE INDEPENDENT LABORATORIES SHOW THAT HE WAS POISONED BY A NOVICHOK-TYPE NERVE AGENT SIMILAR TO THE SUBSTANCE USED AGAINST FORMER RUSSIAN SPY SERGEI SKRIPAL IN 2018.

ON 7 SEPTEMBER, DOCTORS BROUGHT NAVALNY OUT OF THE MEDICALLY INDUCED COMA THEY HAD PLACED HIM IN.

ON 14 SEPTEMBER, NAVALNY WAS TAKEN OFF THE VENTILATOR AND WAS ABLE TO GET OUT OF BED.

ON 15 SEPTEMBER, NAVALNY POSTED A PICTURE FROM HIS HOSPITAL BED ON SOCIAL MEDIA FOR THE FIRST TIME SINCE HIS POISONING.

ON 22 SEPTEMBER, THE DOCTORS AT THE CHARITÉ HOSPITAL DECLARED HIM WELL ENOUGH TO BE DISCHARGED FROM IN-PATIENT CARE.

NAVALNY ASSERTED THAT PUTIN MUST HAVE BEEN BEHIND HIS POISONING, AS ONLY THREE PEOPLE WOULD HAVE BEEN ABLE TO ORDER THE USE OF NOVICHOK...

...THE DIRECTOR OF FSB, THE HEAD OF THE FOREIGN INTELLIGENCE SERVICE, OR THE DIRECTOR OF GUR. NONE OF THESE MEN COULD MAKE THIS DECISION WITHOUT PUTIN'S DIRECT ORDERS.

NAVALNY SAID THAT HE FELT FINE WHEN HE GOT ON THE PLANE. THE FEELING THAT THERE WAS SOMETHING TERRIBLY WRONG WITH HIS BODY CAME ON SUDDENLY.

THERE ARE NO EXISTING WORDS TO DESCRIBE WHAT HAPPENED TO HIM, HE SAID. NOVICHOK ATTACKS THE NERVOUS SYSTEM SO THAT STEP BY STEP, HE LOST THE ABILITY TO BREATHE.

HE COULD STILL WALK, TALK AND SEE, BUT IT WAS EXTREMELY DIFFICULT. FIFTEEN MINUTES LATER, HE KNEW HE WAS DYING.

ON 21 DECEMBER 2020, NAVALNY RELEASED A VIDEO THAT SHOWED HIM IMPERSONATING A RUSSIAN SECURITY OFFICIAL, IN ORDER TO SPEAK BY PHONE WITH A MAN WHO WAS IDENTIFIED AS A CHEMICAL WEAPONS EXPERT, NAMED KONSTANTIN KUDRYAVTSEV.

NAVALNY POSED AS AN AIDE TO THE SECRETARY OF RUSSIA'S SECURITY COUNCIL NIKOLAI PATRUSHEV, PRETENDING TO DEBRIEF KUDRYAVTSEV ABOUT THE OPERATION AND ASKING FOR DETAILS OF WHY THE MISSION HAD FAILED.

KUDRYAVTSEV SAID THAT THE POISON HAD BEEN IN NAVALNY'S CLOTHING, AND ESPECIALLY CONCENTRATED IN HIS UNDERWEAR. NAVALNY WOULD HAVE DIED, HE SAID, IF NOT FOR THE PLANE'S EMERGENCY LANDING AND QUICK RESPONSE FROM AN AMBULANCE CREW ON THE RUNWAY.

ON 17 JANUARY 2021, AFTER ALMOST [FI]VE MONTHS RECUPERATING IN GERMANY, [N]AVALNY RETURNED TO RUSSIA, KNOWING [F]ULL WELL HE WOULD BE ARRESTED ON ARRIVAL.

HIS PLANE, WHICH WAS ORIGINALLY HEADED FOR MOSCOW'S VNUKOVO AIRPORT, WAS DIVERTED TO THE CAPITAL'S SHEREMETYEVO AIRPORT SHORTLY BEFORE IT LANDED.

THIS DIVERSION WAS MADE TO AVOID [M]EDIA SCRUTINY AND THE HUNDREDS OF [P]EOPLE WHO HAD DEFIED A WARNING FROM [T]HE MOSCOW PROSECUTOR'S OFFICE TO WELCOME NAVALNY BACK.

AT PASSPORT CONTROL, NAVALNY WAS DETAINED, ACCORDING TO THE FEDERAL PENITENTIARY SERVICE, FOR 'VIOLATING THE TERMS OF HIS PROBATION BY LEAVING RUSSIA.'

HE WAS ULTIMATELY SENTENCED TO THREE AND A HALF YEARS IN PRISON ON AN EMBEZZLEMENT CHARGE. A CRIME COMMONLY USED BY THE PUTIN REGIME AS A PRETEXT TO JAIL OPPONENTS.

AT THE TIME OF WRITING, NAVALNY IS STILL INCARCERATED, BUT PHYSICALLY WEAK AFTER A 24-DAY HUNGER STRIKE THAT BROUGHT HIM CLOSE TO DEATH.

IS ALEXEI NAVALNY A PARAGON OF LIBERAL VIRTUE? FAR FROM IT. IN THE PAST HE HAS EXPRESSED RACIST OPINIONS.

IN A 2007 PRO-GUN RIGHTS VIDEO, HE PRESENTED HIMSELF AS A 'CERTIFIED NATIONALIST' WHO APPEARED TO COMPARE MUSLIMS TO 'FLIES AND COCKROACHES' — WHILE BEARDED MUSLIM MEN APPEARED IN CUTAWAYS.

SHORTLY BEFORE RELEASING THIS VIDEO, NAVALNY WAS KICKED OUT OF YABLOKO, RUSSIA'S OLDEST LIBERAL DEMOCRATIC PARTY...

...FOR HIS 'NATIONALIST VIEWS' AND BECAUSE OF HIS PARTICIPATION IN THE RUSSIAN MARCH, AN ANNUAL RALLY OF THOUSANDS OF FAR-RIGHT NATIONALISTS AND WHITE SUPREMACISTS.

THE PARTICIPANTS OF THE RUSSIAN MARCHES RALLIED AGAINST THE INFLUX OF LABOUR MIGRANTS FROM EX-SOVIET CENTRAL ASIA AND RUSSIA'S MOSTLY MUSLIM NORTHERN CAUCASUS REGION.

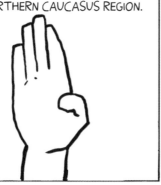

AFTER 2013 NAVALNY STOPPED ATTENDING RUSSIAN MARCHES AND TONED DOWN HIS NATIONALIST RHETORIC. IT'S AT THIS POINT HE BEGAN FOCUSING ON ANTI-CORRUPTION INVESTIGATIONS.

ANTI-CORRUPTION FOUNDATION.

IS NAVALNY WORTH SUPPORTING DESPITE HIS ABHORRENT VIEWS? YES, BECAUSE IT'S NOT NAVALNY VS PUTIN. IT'S DEMOCRACY VS AUTHORITARIANISM. IF INTERNATIONAL ATTENTION REMAINS FOCUSED ONLY ON THE PERSON RATHER THAN THE PROTEST MOVEMENT, THIS WILL HINDER THE DEVELOPMENT OF AN OPPOSITION MOVEMENT IN RUSSIA AND...

...INHIBIT THE DEMOCRATIC WORLD'S RESPONSE TO PUTIN'S AUTHORITARIANISM. FURTHERMORE, AS ODIOUS AS NAVALNY'S PAST WHITE-NATIONALISTIC STATEMENTS ARE, HIS ANTI-CORRUPTION FOUNDATION STILL DOES USEFUL WORK IN EXPOSING THE CRIMINALITY OF THE PUTIN REGIME.

FOR EXAMPLE, TWO DAYS AFTER NAVALNY WAS ARRESTED, THE ANTI-CORRUPTION FOUNDATION RELEASED A VIDEO CALLED 'PUTIN'S PALACE. HISTORY OF THE WORLD'S LARGEST BRIBE.'

NAVALNY ALLEGED THAT AN OPULENT PROPERTY NEAR GELENDZHIK, A TOWN ON THE BLACK SEA COAST, WAS CONSTRUCTED WITH $1.35 BILLION OF ILLICIT FUNDS...

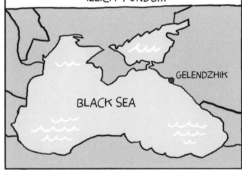

...AND THAT THE OWNER OF THIS PALACE IS VLADIMIR PUTIN.

THE PALACE'S FEATURES INCLUDE A PORT, VINEYARDS, A CHURCH, AN UNDERGROUND HOCKEY RINK, A GREENHOUSE, TWIN HELIPADS...

...AN AMPHITHEATRE, A GUEST HOUSE, AND A TUNNEL THAT GIVES ACCESS TO THE BEACH.

INSIDE THE MAIN BUILDING ARE A SWIMMING POOL, SAUNAS, TURKISH BATHS, A 'MUD' WAREHOUSE, A READING ROOM, A MUSIC LOUNGE AND A CINEMA, A WINE CELLAR, ABOUT A DOZEN GUEST BEDROOMS...

...A HOOKAH BAR WITH A RETRACTABLE STRIPPER POLE, A PERSONAL CASINO, A VIDEO GAME ARCADE, AND A SPECIAL ROOM TO PLAY WITH TOY CARS.

THE ESTATE IS NEARLY FOUR TIMES THE SIZE OF NEARBY GELENDZHIK, A RESORT TOWN OF 50,000 PEOPLE. IT IS SHIELDED FROM SCRUTINY BY A NO-FLY ZONE AND SURROUNDED BY A MARITIME BUFFER ZONE.

PUTIN HAS DENIED OWNERSHIP OF THE PALACE.

NONE OF WHAT IS LISTED THERE [IS MY] PROPERTY, NEITHER ME, NOR MY CLOSE RELATIVES. NEVER!

THE VIDEO CLOSES WITH A DETAILED OUTLINE OF THE SHELL COMPANIES CONNECTED TO PUTIN'S ASSOCIATES — AS WELL AS FAMILY MEMBERS AND MISTRESSES — AND MAKES A STRONG CASE THAT PUTIN IS, SECRETLY, THE WORLD'S RICHEST PERSON.

HOW RICH IS VLADIMIR PUTIN? IT'S IMPOSSIBLE TO KNOW FOR SURE. BUT AS THE PUTIN CRIME CARTEL HAS NOW BEEN PLUNDERING RUSSIA'S WEALTH FOR MORE THAN 20 YEARS, THE ANSWER HAS TO BE IN THE BILLIONS.

HEDGE FUND MANAGER BILL BROWDER, WHOSE FIRM WAS ONCE THE LARGEST PORTFOLIO INVESTOR IN RUSSIA, MADE THIS CLAIM WHEN TESTIFYING TO THE US CONGRESS IN 2017.

I ESTIMATE THAT [PUTIN] HAS ACCUMULATED $200 BILLION OF ILL-GOTTEN GAINS.

WHICH WOULD MAKE PUTIN WEALTHIER THAN THE FOUR OFFICIALLY RICHEST MEN IN THE WORLD: JEFF BEZOS, ELON MUSK, BERNARD ARNAULT AND BILL GATES.

EVERYTHING THAT BELONGS TO THE TERRITORY OF THE RUSSIAN FEDERATION PUTIN CONSIDERS TO BE HIS.

EXILED RUSSIAN BANKER SERGEI PUGACHEV

ANY ATTEMPT TO CALCULATE [HIS NET WORTH] WON'T SUCCEED. HE'S THE RICHEST PERSON IN THE WORLD UNTIL HE LEAVES POWER.

THERE ARE APPROXIMATELY 10,000 OFFICIALS IN RUSSIA WORKING FOR PUTIN WHO ARE GIVEN INSTRUCTIONS TO KILL, TORTURE, KIDNAP, EXTORT MONEY FROM PEOPLE, AND SEIZE THEIR PROPERTY.

THERE IS NOT A SINGLE PENNY REGISTERED IN HIS NAME. IT'S REGISTERED IN OTHER PEOPLE'S NAMES.

MANY OF THESE MONEY HOLDERS APPEAR TO BE PEOPLE HE WAS CLOSE TO BEFORE BECOMING PRESIDENT. SUCH AS PUTIN'S CHILDHOOD FRIEND, PETER KOLBIN. THE FORMER BUTCHER LIVES A QUIET LIFE AND DENIES BEING A BUSINESSMAN.

YET, SOMEHOW, HE IS A SHAREHOLDER OF A COMPANY THAT HAS, IN THE PAST, TRADED ABOUT ONE-THIRD OF ALL RUSSIAN OIL.

OR SERGEI ROLDUGIN, A CELLIST AND ONE OF PUTIN'S OLDEST FRIENDS - HIS DAUGHTER MARIA'S GODFATHER. ROLDUGIN ALSO CLAIMS NOT TO BE A BUSINESSMAN...

...BUT THE PANAMA PAPERS (A LEAK OF 11.5M FILES FROM THE DATABASE OF THE WORLD'S FOURTH BIGGEST OFFSHORE LAW FIRM, MOSSACK FONSECA) SHOWED THAT THE MUSICIAN WITH THE SECOND-HAND CELLO HAD COMPANIES THROUGH WHICH TWO BILLION DOLLARS FLOWED.

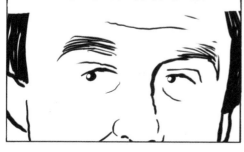

BROWDER CALLS PEOPLE LIKE KOLBIN AND ROLDUGIN 'NOMINEES' WHO ONLY FORMALLY OWN ALL THESE ASSETS, BUT IN FACT...

IT'S PUTIN'S PERSONAL MONEY.

MUCH OF THE PUTIN CRIME CARTEL MONEY IS KEPT OUTSIDE RUSSIA. ACCORDING TO A GLOBAL FINANCIAL INTEGRITY AND A NATIONAL BUREAU OF ECONOMIC RESEARCH STUDY, TOTAL PRIVATE RUSSIAN HOLDINGS ABROAD ARE ASSESSED IN THE RANGE OF $800 BILLION TO $1.3 TRILLION.

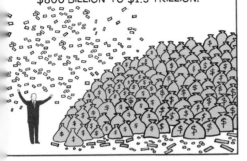

VAST AMOUNTS OF RUSSIAN OFFSHORE WEALTH FLOW THROUGH TWO COUNTRIES IN PARTICULAR: THE US AND THE UK, BECAUSE, UNLIKE MOST OTHER COUNTRIES, THEY ALLOW ANONYMOUS INVESTMENT IN REAL ESTATE ON A LARGE SCALE.

I'D LIKE TO BUY ENORMOUS AMOUNTS OF LONDON, PLEASE.

IN 2015, THE US TREASURY ESTIMATED THAT $300 BILLION A YEAR WAS LAUNDERED IN THE UNITED STATES. THE US GOVERNMENT DETECTS A MERE 0.1 PER CENT OF THAT MONEY. A MINUSCULE AMOUNT.

I'D LIKE TO BUY ENORMOUS AMOUNTS OF NEW YORK, PLEASE.

THE REASON FOR THIS IS THAT ANONYMOUS COMPANIES ARE ALLOWED TO INVEST IN THE US, WHICH MAKES THE SOURCE OF THE MONEY ALMOST IMPOSSIBLE TO DISCOVER.

FOR SALE

THE SAME IS TRUE IN BRITAIN, WHERE THE NATIONAL CRIME AGENCY ESTIMATES THAT $125 BILLION IS LAUNDERED EACH YEAR.

FOR SALE

BEN JUDAH HAS SAID THAT PUTIN'S REGIME IS CENTRED AROUND MONEY LAUNDERING. THE REDISTRIBUTION OF STOLEN ASSETS IN WAYS THAT ARE CLOSELY INTEGRATED INTO THE WORLD FINANCIAL SYSTEM.

BILL BROWDER BELIEVES THIS IS WHERE PUTIN'S REGIME IS MOST VULNERABLE. HIS CRUCIAL INSIGHT IS THAT BY DENYING PUTIN AND HIS CROOKED FRIENDS ACCESS TO OUR ECONOMIES, WE COULD CRIPPLE THEIR ABILITY TO STEAL AND WEAKEN THEM AT HOME AND ABROAD.

BROWDER, A BRITISH CITIZEN, LIVED IN MOSCOW FOR TEN YEARS AND IN THAT TIME WAS AMONG THE MOST SIGNIFICANT INVESTORS IN RUSSIAN BUSINESS. HIS FUND, HERMITAGE CAPITAL, REACHED A VALUATION OF $4.5 BILLION.

BROWDER'S RESPONSE TO THE CORRUPTION HE FOUND IN RUSSIA WAS TO BECOME AN ACTIVIST SHAREHOLDER AND TAKE ON LARGE RUSSIAN COMPANIES SUCH AS GAZPROM, SURGUTNEFTEGAZ, UNIFIED ENERGY SYSTEMS, AND SIDANCO.

IN 2005, AFTER SPENDING A WEEKEND VISITING FAMILY IN LONDON, HE WAS DETAINED AT MOSCOW'S SHEREMETYEVO AIRPORT... AND THEN DEPORTED.

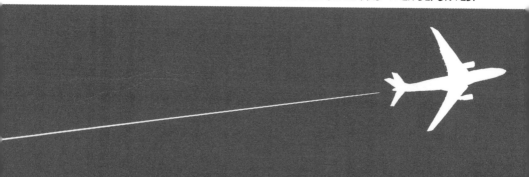

SOON AFTERWARDS, BROWDER'S VISA WAS REVOKED AND HE WAS PLACED ON A LIST OF PEOPLE CONSIDERED A THREAT TO NATIONAL SECURITY. FOLLOWING HIS EXPULSION, THE RUSSIAN AUTHORITIES RAIDED HIS OFFICES, SEIZED HERMITAGE FUND'S INVESTMENT COMPANIES AND USED THEM TO STEAL $230 MILLION OF TAXES THAT HERMITAGE HAD ALREADY PAID.

MOST HERMITAGE STAFF FLED ABROAD BUT SERGEI MAGNITSKY, LAWYER AND TAX AUDITOR, STAYED IN MOSCOW AND FIGURED OUT THE SCAM.

THE OFFICIALS HE ACCUSED HAD HIM ARRESTED AND THROWN IN JAIL, WHERE PRISON GUARDS BEAT HIM. HE DIED IN CUSTODY IN 2009 AFTER BEING REFUSED MEDICAL TREATMENT.

THIS SET IN MOTION BROWDER'S CRUSADE. THE SERGEI MAGNITSKY RULE OF LAW ACCOUNTABILITY ACT WAS PASSED IN THE US IN 2012.

SINCE THEN, PUTIN HAS MADE IT PERHAPS HIS LARGEST FOREIGN PRIORITY TO HAVE THE MAGNITSKY ACT REPEALED. BUT NONE OF HIS EFFORTS HAVE WORKED. NOT ONLY HAS IT NOT BEEN REPEALED, IT'S SPREAD TO SIX ADDITIONAL COUNTRIES, INCLUDING THE UNITED KINGDOM, CANADA AND GIBRALTAR.

THE ACT PROHIBITS NAMED INDIVIDUALS, SUCH AS THOSE INVOLVED IN THE MURDER OF SERGEI MAGNITSKY, FROM ENTERING THE TERRITORY OF THE COUNTRIES THAT SIGN THEM INTO LAW, AND FREEZE THEIR ASSETS WHENEVER THEY ARE DETECTED. THE EU ADOPTED A MAGNITSKY LAW IN DECEMBER 2020, AND YET MORE COUNTRIES ARE CONSIDERING THEIR OWN MAGNITSKY ACTS, INCLUDING AUSTRALIA.

I'D LIKE MY MONEY AND PROPERTY.

NOPE

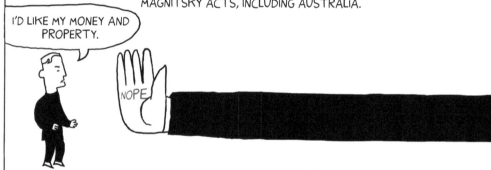

THIS SHOULD BE ONLY THE BEGINNING. BOTH THE UK AND THE US NEED TO CONSIDER THE DAMAGE DONE WHEN THEY ALLOW ANONYMOUS COMPANIES, MANY OF THEM RUSSIAN, TO LAUNDER MONEY IN THEIR COUNTRIES. GREED SHOULD NOT DICTATE POLICY OR OVERRIDE MORAL PRINCIPLES.

IT IS LONG PAST TIME THERE WAS A CONCERTED EFFORT TO PUNISH THE KREMLIN FOR ITS VIOLATIONS OF HUMAN RIGHTS AND REPRESSION OF OPPONENTS BOTH AT HOME AND ABROAD.

THE WORLD NEEDS TO STOP PRETENDING THAT PUTIN'S REGIME IS A NORMAL STATE. PUTIN AND HIS CRIMINAL CRONIES ARE DESERVING OF THE MOST CRUSHING SANCTIONS AND POLITICAL ISOLATION FOR ALL THEIR HUMAN RIGHTS CRIMES, ASSASSINATIONS, CYBER ATTACKS, ATTACKS ON WESTERN COUNTRIES, DISINFORMATION CAMPAIGNS, AND THE ILLEGAL ANNEXATION OF UKRAINE.

RUSSIA TODAY IS A WHITE-IDENTITY SOCIETY THAT CRUSHES OPPOSITION, WRAPS ITSELF IN NOSTALGIA, RUNS RIGGED ELECTIONS THAT PROVIDE A VENEER OF DEMOCRACY WITHOUT THE RISK, AND ALLOWS THE WEALTHY AND POWERFUL BRUTAL CONTROL.

WESTERN POLITICIANS WHO MAKE EXCUSES FOR PUTIN, OR REFUSE TO SEE HIS CRIMINAL BEHAVIOUR, ARE AT BEST NAIVE, AND AT WORST COMPLICIT IN THAT CRIMINALITY. PUTIN SHOULD BE CALLED OUT FOR WHO HE IS.

HE SHOULD NOT BE CONSIDERED AN INTERNATIONALLY RESPECTED LEADER, BUT A MURDEROUS KGB MAFIA BOSS WITH AN ASSASSINATION SQUAD AND A CHEMICAL WEAPONS LAB.

DICTATORS DON'T ASK WHY, THEY ASK WHY NOT. ENGAGING OR IGNORING THEM HAS ONLY ENCOURAGED THEM TO ATTACK. STANDING UP TO AUTHORITARIANS IS THE ONLY WAY TO PROTECT DEMOCRACY AT HOME AND ABROAD.

GARRY KASPAROV
RUSSIAN CHESS GRANDMASTER
AND POLITICAL COMMENTOR

PUTIN EMPOWERS THUGS AROUND THE WORLD BY OFFERING THEM SUPPORT. HIS SUCCESS ENCOURAGES OTHERS TO ROLL BACK FREEDOMS IN THEIR OWN COUNTRIES. WITHOUT PUTIN, THEY WOULD BE FAR MORE LIKELY TO FALL AND THEREFORE MORE WORRIED ABOUT REPERCUSSIONS FOR BRUTALITY. PUNISHING PUTIN HELPS PROMOTE DEMOCRACY.

MURDER AND CORRUPTION SHOULD BE PUNISHED, NEVER REWARDED. EITHER WE SUPPORT DEMOCRACY, FREEDOM OF SPEECH AND THE RULE OF LAW EVERYWHERE, OR WE WILL SEE THESE VALUES WITHER AWAY.

DO NOTHING AND PUTIN WILL STRENGTHEN HIS GRIP ON OUR WORLD. TAKE ACTION AND WE WE WILL BOTH ENCOURAGE THE STIRRINGS OF DEMOCRACY IN RUSSIA, *AND* STOP HIS REGIME SPREADING CORRUPTION TO OTHER COUNTRIES, INCLUDING OUR OWN.

IT'S A SIMPLE CHOICE. DEMOCRACY OR DICTATORSHIP? THE CHOICE IS UP TO US.

ACKNOWLEDGEMENTS:

I find myself writing the same thing in the acknowledgements of every book, but it's always true. I'm indebted to the many journalists whose work I've drawn from while writing/drawing this book. This time I'm particularly indebted to *Winter Is Coming* by Garry Kasparov, *Putin's People* by Catherine Belton, *The Man Without a Face* by Masha Gessen and *We Need to Talk About Putin* by Mark Galeotti. These books are essential reading if you want to explore the subjects of Putin and Russia in greater detail.

Thanks are also due to Virpi Oinonen, Anna and Andy Miller, Bryan Talbot, Robin Ince, Eileen Gunn and the Royal Literary Fund, Jonathan Edwards, Louise Evans, Jo Ingold, Nicola Toms, Avid Stan, Gil Roth, Helen Clarke, Pete Ashton, Stephen Holland and Jonathan Rigby at Page 45, Jared Myland at OK Comics, Selina Lock, Stephen Weiner, Lizz Lunney, Joseph Hewitt, Steven Mortiboy, Jim Dougan, Michael Green, Scott McCloud, MK Czerwiec, Patricia Fraser, Adam Hibberd, Marion Millard, Samantha McDermott, James Langdell, Reuben Willmott, Jeet Heer, and Garry Barker.

Thanks to Candida Lacey at Myriad Editions. A special thanks to editor, Corinne Pearlman and copy editor Vicki Heath-Silk, for the colossal amount of work they did on this book.

And most of all to Bonnie Millard for her constant and unwavering love and support.

REFERENCES :

BOOKS

Putin V. *First Person: An Astonishingly Frank Self-Portrait by Russia's President.* PublicAffairs (Perseus Books): United States; 2000.

Kasparov G. *Winter Is Coming: Why Vladimir Putin and the Enemies of the Free World Must Be Stopped.* Atlantic Books: London; 2015.

Belton C. *Putin's People: How the KGB Took Back Russia and then Took on the West.* William Collins (Harper Collins Publishers): London; 2020.

Myers SL. *The New Tsar: The Rise and Reign of Vladimir Putin.* Simon & Schuster: London; 2015.

Gessen M. *The Man Without a Face: The Unlikely Rise of Vladimir Putin.* Granta: London; 2013.

Galeotti M. *We Need to Talk About Putin: How the West Gets Him Wrong.* Ebury Press (Penguin Books): London; 2019.

Yeltsin B. *Against the Grain: An Autobiography.* Simon & Schuster: United States; 1990.

Vaksberg A (translated McGregor P).*Toxic Politics: The Secret History of the Kremlin's Poison Laboratory – from the Special Cabinet to the Death of Litvinenko.* Praeger (ABC-CLIO: United States; 2011.

Judah B. *Fragile Empire, How Russia Fell In and Out of Love with Vladimir Putin.* Yale University Press: United States; 2013.

Patrikarakos D. *War in 140 Characters: How Social Media is Reshaping Conflict in the 21st Century.* Basic Books (Hachette Book Group): New York; 2017.

Weissmann A. *Where Law Ends: Inside the Mueller Investigation.* Random House (Penguin Random House): United States; 2020.

WEBSITES: RISE TO POWER

Berger M, Boris N. Yeltsin, Reformer Who Broke Up the U.S.S.R., Dies at 76. *The New York Times.* 2007 April 24. https://www.nytimes.com/2007/04/24/world/europe/24yeltsin.html (accessed 2020 January 3).

Nadler G. Yeltsin Reflects on Drinking, Lewinsky Scandal. *ABC News.* 2006 January 6. https://abcnews.go.com/International/story?id=82447&page=1 (accessed 2020 January 4).

Harding L. Marina Salye obituary. *The Guardian.* 2012 March 28. https://www.theguardian.com/world/2012/mar/28/marina-salye (accessed 2020 January 4).

Belton C. The inside story of how Putin and his KGB cronies took control of Russia. *The Sunday Times.* 2020 March 29. https://www.thetimes.co.uk/article/the-inside-story-of-how-putin-and-his-kgb-cronies-took-control-of-russia-prknjjhgh (accessed 2020 January 7).

Opponent of Putin shot dead outside his flat. *The Irish Times.* 2003 April 18. https://www.irishtimes.com/news/opponent-of-putin-shot-dead-outside-his-flat-1.356097 (accessed 2020 January 10).

Gessen M. The best theory for explaining the mysterious death of Putin's mentor. *Business Insider.* 2015 February 17. https://www.businessinsider.com/the-mysterious-death-of-putins-mentor-2015-2?r=US&IR=T (accessed 2020 February 25).

Salter L, Lopez L, and Kakoyiannis A. How the 1999 Russian apartment bombings led to Putin's rise to power. *Business Insider.*

2021 April 7. https://www.businessinsider.com/how-the-1999-russian-apartment-bombings-led-to-putins-rise-to-power-2018-3?r=US&IR=T (accessed 2021 April 10).

Mizokami K. The True Story of the Russian Kursk Submarine Disaster. *Popular Mechanics.* 2018 September 28. https://www.popularmechanics.com/military/navy-ships/a23494010/kursk-submarine-disaster (accessed 2021 April 18).

Traynor I. Putin aims Kursk fury at media. *The Guardian.* 2000 August 25. https://www.theguardian.com/world/2000/aug/25/kursk.russia2 (accessed 2021 June 7).

ALEXANDER LITVINENKO POISONING

Dejevsky M. The weird world of Boris Berezovsky: Alexander Litvinenko's inquest has provided an intriguing insight into the dead tycoon. *The Independent.* 2015 March 18. https://www.independent.co.uk/news/world/europe/weird-world-boris-berezovsky-alexander-litvinenko-s-inquest-has-provided-intriguing-insight-dead-tycoon-10117927.html (accessed 2021 April 23).

Starobin P. My Lunch With Litvinenko. *The Atlantic.* December 2006. https://www.theatlantic.com/magazine/archive/2006/12/my-lunch-with-litvinenko/305472 (accessed 2020 February 2).

Encyclopaedia Britannica. Mikhail Gorbachev president of Soviet Union. 2021 March 16. https://www.britannica.com/biography/Mikhail-Gorbachev (accessed 2021 June 3).

Ray M. Mikhail Khodorkovsky Russian businessman. *Encyclopaedia Britannica.* 2020 June 22. https://www.britannica.com/biography/Mikhail-Khodorkovsky (accessed 2020 February 3).

Ferris-Rotman A. Britain regrets Russia's Lugovoy elected to Duma *Reuters.* 2007 December 7. https://www.reuters.com/article/us-russia-britain-lugovoy/britain-regrets-russias-lugovoy-elected-to-duma-idUSL0749585820071207 (accessed 2021 June 6).

HC Deb. Litvinenko Inquiry – in the House of Commons. *They Work For You.* 2016 January 21. https://www.theyworkforyou.com/debates/?id=2016-01-21b.1569.0#g1578.0 (accessed 2021 June 6).

BBC. Alexander Litvinenko: Profile of murdered Russian spy. 2016 January 21. https://www.bbc.co.uk/news/uk-19647226 (accessed 2021 June 6).

Dow Jones & Company. Poisonous Chain of Events. *The Wall Street Journal Online.* 2006. http://www.wsj.com/public/resources/documents/info-russspy06-time.html?printVersion=true (accessed 2020 February 22).

Harding L. Alexander Litvinenko and the most radioactive towel in history. *The Guardian.* 2016 March 6. https://www.theguardian.com/world/2016/mar/06/alexander-litvinenko-and-the-most-radioactive-towel-in-history (accessed 2020 February 22).

MacGill M (medically reviewed by Biggers A). Polonium-210: Why is Po-210 so dangerous? *Medical News Today.* 2017 July 28. https://www.medicalnewstoday.com/articles/58088 (accessed 2020 February 22).

MOSCOW THEATRE SIEGE

Daniszewski J. First Fatality of the Crisis a Would-Be Good Samaritan. *Los Angeles Times.* 2002 October 26. https://www.latimes.com/archives/la-xpm-2002-oct-26-fg-victim26-story.html

ccessed 2020 February 11).

C. Hostages speak of storming terror. 2002 October 26. http://news.
c.co.uk/1/hi/world/europe/2363679.stm (accessed 2021 June 6).

echetnikov A. Moscow theatre siege: Questions remain
answered. *BBC News*. 2012 October 24. https://www.bbc.co.uk/
ws/world-europe-20067384 (accessed 2021 June 6).

Jazeera. Siege victims blame Russian authorities. 2003 October
). https://www.aljazeera.com/news/2003/10/20/siege-victims-
ame-russian-authorities (accessed 2021 June 6).

ESLAN SCHOOL SIEGE

homami N, and agencies. Russia could have done more to
revent Beslan school siege, court finds. *The Guardian*. 2017 April
3. https://www.theguardian.com/world/2017/apr/13/russia-
uld-have-done-more-to-prevent-beslan-school-siege-court-finds
ccessed 2020 February 13).

he Guardian, and agencies. Timeline: the Beslan school siege.
004 September 6. https://www.theguardian.com/world/2004/
p/06/schoolsworldwide.chechnya (accessed 2020 February 17).

NACCOUNTABLE DEATHS

olitkovskaya A. Poisoned by Putin. *The Guardian*. 2004 September
. https://www.theguardian.com/world/2004/sep/09/russia.media
ccessed 2021 June 6).

imon S. Why Do Russian Journalists Keep Falling? *NPR*. 2018
pril 21. https://www.npr.org/2018/04/21/604497554/why-do-
ussian-journalists-keep-falling?t=1618154765917 (accessed
020 February 17).

he Associated Press. A List of Murdered Russian Journalists That
Moscow Says It Didn't Kill. *Haaretz*. 2018 May 30. https://www.
aaretz.com/world-news/europe/a-list-of-murdered-russian-
ournalists-that-moscow-says-it-didn-t-kill-1.6133887 (accessed
020 February 17).

Harding L. Colleagues urge investigation into Russian journalist's
death. *The Guardian*. 2009 December 1. https://www.theguardian.
com/world/2009/dec/01/olga-kotovskaya-journalist-death-
kaliningrad (accessed 2020 February 17).

UKRAINIAN & SYRIAN WARS

Keating J. Interview: Boris Nemtsov. *Foreign Policy*. 2010 March
1. https://foreignpolicy.com/2010/03/01/interview-boris-nemtsov
(accessed 2021 June 6).

Yaffa J. The Unaccountable Death of Boris Nemtsov. *New Yorker*. 2016
February 26. https://www.newyorker.com/news/news-desk/the-
unaccountable-death-of-boris-nemtsov (accessed 2020 March 4).

Human Rights Watch. Russia: New Anti-Gay Crackdown in
Chechnya. Police Detain, Torture Men in Grozny. 2019 May 8.
https://www.hrw.org/news/2019/05/08/russia-new-anti-gay-
crackdown-chechnya (accessed 2020 March 5).

BBC. MH17 Ukraine plane crash: What we know. 2020 February 26.
https://www.bbc.co.uk/news/world-europe-28357880 (accessed
2020 March 6).

NL Times. JIT: MH17 shot down with missile fired from pro-Russian
rebel controlled field. 2016 September 28. https://nltimes.

nl/2016/09/28/jit-mh17-shot-missile-fired-pro-russian-rebel-
controlled-field (accessed 2021 June 7).

Bond D. Russia a 'formidable adversary', say UK spymasters.
Financial Times. 2017 December 20. https://www.ft.com/content/
ff155500-e5a3-11e7-8b99-0191e45377ec (accessed 2021 June 6).

Dennekamp G. Audio tapes of thousands of overheard
conversations, a reconstruction of the MH17 disaster. *NOS*. April
11. https://nos.nl/nieuwsuur/artikel/2376246-audio-tapes-of-
thousands-of-overheard-conversations-a-reconstruction-of-the-
mh17-disaster.html (accessed 2021 April 11).

Solon O. How Syria's White Helmets became victims of an online
propaganda machine. *The Guardian*. 2017 December 18. https://
www.theguardian.com/world/2017/dec/18/syria-white-helmets-
conspiracy-theories (accessed 2020 March 28).

Rahman-Jones I. Why does Russia support Syria and President
Assad? *BBC News*. 2017 April 11. https://www.bbc.co.uk/news/
newsbeat-39554171 (accessed 2020 March 10).

The New Arab, and agencies. Cost of Syria war destruction almost
$400 billion, UN estimates. 2018 August 9. *The New Arab*. https://
english.alaraby.co.uk/english/news/2018/8/8/cost-of-syria-war-
destruction-almost-400-billion-un (accessed 2020 March 10).

McKernan B. OPCW report set to blame Syria chemical attacks
on Bashar al-Assad. *The Guardian*. 2020 April 6. https://www.
theguardian.com/world/2020/apr/06/report-set-to-blame-syria-
chemical-attacks-on-bashar-al-assad (accessed 2020 April 6).

Alami M. Russia's disinformation campaign has changed how
we see Syria. *Atlantic Council*. 2018 September 4. https://www.
atlanticcouncil.org/blogs/syriasource/russia-s-disinformation-
campaign-has-changed-how-we-see-syria (accessed 2021 June 6).

Chulov M. How Syria's disinformation wars destroyed the
co-founder of the White Helmets. *The Guardian*. 2020 October
27. https://www.theguardian.com/news/2020/oct/27/syria-
disinformation-war-white-helmets-mayday-rescue-james-le-
mesurier (accessed 2020 March 28).

Yeung P. Russia committing war crimes by deliberately bombing
civilians and aid workers, says Amnesty International. *The
Independent*. 2016 February 21. https://www.independent.co.uk/
news/world/middle-east/russia-civilians-war-crimes-amnesty-
international-a6887096.html (accessed 2020 March 28).

TRUMP & RUSSIA

Mayer J. How Russia Helped Swing the Election for Trump.
New Yorker. 2018 September 24. https://www.newyorker.com/
magazine/2018/10/01/how-russia-helped-to-swing-the-election-
for-trump (accessed 2020 June 1).

CNN Editorial Research. 2016 Presidential Campaign Hacking Fast
Facts. *CNN*. 2020 October 28. https://edition.cnn.com/2016/12/26/
us/2016-presidential-campaign-hacking-fast-facts/index.html
(accessed 2021 June 6).

Kiely E, Gore D. In His Own Words: Trump on Russian Meddling.
FactCheck (Annenberg Public Policy Center). 2018 February
19. https://www.factcheck.org/2018/02/words-trump-russian-
meddling (accessed 2020 June 1).

DHS Press Office. Joint Statement from the Department of Homeland Security and Office of the Director of National Intelligence on Election Security. *DHS*. 2016 October 7. https://www.dhs.gov/news/2016/10/07/joint-statement-department-homeland-security-and-office-director-national (accessed 2020 June 1).

BBC. Trump Russia affair: Key questions answered. 2019 July 24. https://www.bbc.co.uk/news/world-us-canada-42493918 (accessed 2020 June 1).

Levine M. The Russia probe: A timeline from Moscow to Mueller. *ABC News*. 2019 July 23. https://abcnews.go.com/Politics/russia-probe-timeline-moscow-mueller/story?id=57427441 (accessed 2020 June 1).

Pengelly M. Mueller too timid in Trump-Russia investigation, top prosecutor claims. *The Guardian*. 2020 September 22. https://www.theguardian.com/us-news/2020/sep/22/mueller-timid-trump-russia-investigation-prosecutor-andrew-weissmann (accessed 2020 September 22).

Friedman D, Corn D. With His Pardons of Stone and Manafort, Trump Completes His Cover-Up. *Mother Jones*. 2020 December 23. https://www.motherjones.com/politics/2020/12/with-his-pardons-of-stone-and-manafort-trump-completes-his-cover-up (accessed 2020 December 23).

Savage M. Trump told Theresa May he doubted Russia was behind Skripal poisoning. *The Guardian*. 2019 October 5. https://www.theguardian.com/us-news/2019/oct/05/trump-told-theresa-may-he-doubted-russia-was-behind-skripal-poisoning (accessed 2020 December 1).

Harding L. The Skripal poisonings: the bungled assassination with the Kremlin's fingerprints all over it. *The Guardian*. 2018 December 26. https://www.theguardian.com/news/2018/dec/26/skripal-poisonings-bungled-assassination-kremlin-putin-salisbury (accessed 2020 December 1).

Harding L. 'A chain of stupidity': the Skripal case and the decline of Russia's spy agencies. *The Guardian*. 2020 June 23. https://www.theguardian.com/world/2020/jun/23/skripal-salisbury-poisoning-decline-of-russia-spy-agencies-gru (accessed 2020 December 1).

Smith D. 'The perfect target': Russia cultivated Trump as asset for 40 years – ex-KGB spy. *The Guardian*. 2021 January 29. https://www.theguardian.com/us-news/2021/jan/29/trump-russia-asset-claims-former-kgb-spy-new-book?CMP=Share_iOSApp_Other (accessed 2021 January 29).

STAYING IN POWER

Klimkin P, Ivanov V, and Umland A. Putin's new constitution spells out modern Russia's imperial ambitions. *Atlantic Council*. 2020 September 10. https://www.atlanticcouncil.org/blogs/ukrainealert/putins-new-constitution-spells-out-modern-russias-imperial-ambitions/ (accessed 2021 June 6).

Russell M. Briefing: Constitutional change in Russia: More Putin, or preparing for post-Putin. *European Parliament*. 2020 May. https://www.europarl.europa.eu/RegData/etudes/BRIE/2020/651935/EPRS_BRI(2020)651935_EN.pdf (accessed 2021 June 6).

Bennetts M. Vladimir Putin to get protection from prosecution for life. *The Sunday Times*. 2020 November 6. https://www.thetimes.co.uk/article/vladimir-putin-to-get-protection-from-prosecution-for-life-pkb09rsgq (accessed 2021 February 29).

COVID-19

Chappell B. Russia's Sputnik Vaccine Is Reported To Be 92% Effective Against COVID-19. *NPR*. 2021 February

2. https://www.npr.org/sections/coronavirus-live-updates/2021/02/02/963166648/russias-sputnik-vaccine-is-reported-to-be-92-effective-against-covid-19 (accessed 2021 February 29).

Dyer O. Covid-19: Russia admits to understating deaths by more than two thirds. *The British Medical Journal*. 2020 December 31. https://www.bmj.com/content/371/bmj.m4975 (accessed 2021 February 29).

Roth A. 'Disinfection tunnel' set up to protect Vladimir Putin from coronavirus. *The Guardian*. 2020 June 17. https://www.theguardian.com/world/2020/jun/17/disinfection-tunnel-vladimir-putin-coronavirus-russia (accessed 2021 February 29).

ALEXEI NAVALNY

Bidder B, Esch C. Russian Opposition Leader Alexei Navalny on His Poisoning: 'I Assert that Putin Was Behind the Crime'. *Spiegel International*. 2020 October 1. https://www.spiegel.de/international/world/alexei-navalny-on-his-poisoning-i-assert-that-putin-was-behind-the-crime-a-ae5923d5-20f3-4117-80bd-39a99b5b86f4 (accessed 2021 June 6).

Gil J. Alexey Navalny: 'I have no doubt that Putin gave the order to poison me'. *El País*. 2020 December 14. https://english.elpais.com/international/2020-12-14/alexei-navalny-i-have-no-doubt-that-putin-gave-the-order-to-poison-me.html (accessed 2021 February 29).

Mirovalev M. Has Alexey Navalny moved on from his nationalist past? *Al Jazeera*. 2021 February 25. https://www.aljazeera.com/news/2021/2/25/navalny-has-the-kremlin-foe-moved-on-from-his-nationalist-past (accessed 2021 March 2).

Roache M. The Inside Story of How Alexey Navalny Uncovered Putin's $1.3 Billion Palace. *Time*. 2021 January 29. https://time.com/5934092/navalny-putin-palace-investigation (accessed 2021 March 19).

PUTIN'S FUTURE

Davis B. Revelations About 'Putin's Palace' Helped Spark Widespread Protests in Russia. Here's What's Inside His Secret 'New Versailles'. *Artnet*. 2021 January 26. https://news.artnet.com/art-world/putins-palace-luxury-1939501 (accessed 2021 June 6).

Hanbury M, Cain Á. No one knows Putin's exact net worth, but many speculate he's the wealthiest person on the planet – his $1 billion palace and $500 million yacht explain why. *Business Insider*. 2018 July 16. https://www.businessinsider.com/how-putin-spends-his-mysterious-fortune-2017-6?r=US&IR=T (accessed 2021 March 19).

Yaffa J. How Bill Browder Became Russia's Most Wanted Man. *New Yorker*. 2018 August 13. https://www.newyorker.com/magazine/2018/08/20/how-bill-browder-became-russias-most-wanted-man (accessed 2021 March 20).

Browder B. I'm Bill Browder. Here's the Biggest Mistake Putin Made When Trying to Get Access to Me Through Trump. *Time*. 2018 July 16. https://time.com/5340545/bill-browder-vladimir-putin-magnitsky-act-donald-trump (accessed 2021 June 6).

Harding L. Who was Sergei Magnitsky and how did UK sanctions come about? *The Guardian*. 2020 July 6. https://www.theguardian.com/politics/2020/jul/06/who-was-sergei-magnitsky-and-how-did-uk-sanctions-come-about (accessed 2021 March 20).